The Divorce Experience of
Working and Middle Class Women

Research in Clinical Psychology, No. 8

Peter E. Nathan, Series Editor
Professor and Chairman
Department of Clinical Psychology
Rutgers, the State University of New Jersey

Other Titles in This Series

No. 1	*Couple Constancy: Conversations with Today's Happily Married People*	Lance T. Laurence
No. 2	*Family and/or Career: Plans of First-Time Mothers*	Debra L. Behrman
No. 3	*The Meaning of Grandparenthood*	Helen Q. Kivnick
No. 4	*Emotional Intimacy in Marriage: A Sex-roles Perspective*	Allison Parelman
No. 5	*Departure from Traditional Roles: Mid-Life Women Break the Daisy Chains*	Rosemary Anastasio Segalla
No. 6	*Coping with Chemotherapy*	Karin E. Ringler
No. 7	*Adolescent Suicidal Behavior: A Family Systems Model*	Roma J. Heillig
No. 9	*Climbing the Ladder of Success in Highheels: Backgrounds of Professional Women*	Jill A. Steinberg
No. 10	*Work and Marriage: The Two-Profession Couple*	Roslyn K. Malmaud
No. 11	*Families of Gifted Children*	Dewey G. Cornell

The Divorce Experience of Working and Middle Class Women

by
Toni L'Hommedieu

UMI RESEARCH PRESS
Ann Arbor, Michigan

Copyright © 1984, 1981
Toni Robin L'Hommedieu
All rights reserved

Produced and distributed by
UMI Research Press
an imprint of
University Microfilms International
Ann Arbor, Michigan 48106

Library of Congress Cataloging in Publication Data

L'Hommedieu, Toni.
   The divorce experience of working and middle class women.

   (Research in clinical psychology ; no. 8)
   Revision of thesis (Ph.D)–University of Pittsburgh, 1981.
   Bibliography: p.
   Includes index.
   1. Divorce–United States–Case studies. 2. Working class women–United States–Attitudes–Case studies. 3. Middle classes–United States–Attitudes–Case studies. 4. Women–United States–Attitudes–Case studies. I. Title. II. Series.

HQ834.L48 1984   306.8'9   83-17967
ISBN 0-8357-1478-0

Contents

Acknowledgments *vii*

Chapter 1 Purpose of the Study *1*
  Introduction
  Background
  Rationale for the Study
  Statement of the Problem

Chapter 2 Review of Related Literature *5*
  Central Themes in the Divorce Experience
    No Reaction to the Final Separation
    Financial Concerns
    Single Parenting Concerns
    Social Concerns
  Resolution of Central Themes
  A Comparison Between the Working Class Marriage and the Middle Class Marriage
    Courtship
    Marital Roles
    Sexuality
    Child Rearing

Chapter 3 Methodology *19*
  Statement of the Problem
  Definition of Terms
  Research Method
  Subjects
  Procedures
    Population Selection
    Pilot Interviews
    Research Interview
    Follow-up Interviews

Analysis of the Data
Limitations
Delimitations

Chapter 4 Results   *29*
Design
Subjects
Data
Descriptive Summaries
General Descriptions

Chapter 5 Conclusions   *97*
Introduction
Research Questions
Discussion
Implications for Counselors and Recommendations for Further Study

Appendix A *125*

Appendix B *127*

Appendix C *145*

Bibliography *161*

Index *165*

Acknowledgments

The completion of this study was the culmination of the combined efforts of several people who gave of their time and energy in emotional and physical support. Gratitude is extended to these people: Dr. Nancy Elman; Dr. David Botwin; Dr. Herbert Barry; Dr. Judith Scott; Dr. Ghassem Shamsi—husband and partner; Kenneth L'Hommedieu Cornell—son; Tod L'Hommedieu Cornell—son; Laila L'Hommedieu Shamsi—daughter; Parveen L'Hommedieu Shamsi—daughter; Kenneth and Nancy L'Hommedieu—parents, confidants, and supporters; Jo-Ann L'Hommedieu Nicholson; Andrea L'Hommedieu; Cynthia L'Hommedieu; Kathy Paternoster and Jean Kandsberger—typists; Judith Aaronson, Ruth Ann Wilner and Dr. Dorothy Gold—editors.

1
Purpose of the Study

Introduction

The purpose of this study is to generate a description of the divorce experience from the perspectives of the working class woman and the middle class woman and to investigate the relationship of socio-economic factors to post-divorce adjustment. This study is based on the following assumptions:

1. that the central themes common to divorced middle class women referred to in the literature are common to divorced working class women also;
2. that the specific pre-divorce conditions associated with the progress of post-divorce resolution of the central themes referred to in the literature for middle class women, exist for working class women also;
3. that socio-economic factors influence the subject's perception of resolutions of central themes in post-divorce adjustment.

Background

A search of the literature reveals that studies on the subject of divorce are limited to the middle class woman's experience of divorce. Studies concerning the divorce experience of working class women do not exist.

In reference to the middle class, the literature describes recurring central themes which develop out of the divorce experience of middle class women. Central themes are those unifying ideas or concerns common to the divorce experience. These central themes are:

1. Intra-personal concerns regarding the emotional reaction to final separation;
2. Financial concerns;
3. Single parenting concerns;
4. Inter-personal concerns.

Purpose of the Study

The resolutions of these central themes are the subject of studies (Goode, 1956, *Women In Transition,* 1975 and Bohannon, 1968) which conclude that specific pre-divorce conditions affect the middle class woman's experience of post-divorce adjustment. These specific pre-divorce conditions are:

1. The subject's perception of her pre-divorce experience of the marriage;
2. The subject's perception of her inner strengths;
3. The subject's perception of her support systems;
4. The subject's perception of her pre-divorce relationships with her children, spouse, family of origin and her in-laws.

Furthermore, these three studies state that middle class women with a high degree of involvement and emotional commitment in the four areas were seen as having a lesser degree of difficulty in the post-divorce adjustment.

Although working class women have not been the subjects for studies concerning divorce, they have been the subjects for studies concerning their perceptions of their roles in marriage and in the family. Rubin (1976) and Komarovsky (1964) conducted studies in the area of working and middle class marriages and families which indicated that socio-economic factors influenced the women's perception of their roles in these two areas.

Therefore, the assumption is made that socio-economic factors will influence the perception of the central themes of divorce and how they are resolved in the post-divorce adjustment.

Rationale for the Study

Statistics dealing with divorce indicate that one out of every three marriages ends in divorce. Statistics also indicate that a higher percentage of divorces occur among the working class than among the middle class. (1974 U.S. Census Report)

Considering the number of divorces among the working class as compared to the middle class, the limited amount of research among the working class creates an obvious and unfortunate void. The assumption cannot be made that the working class experience of divorce mirrors that of the middle class.

The goal of this study, then, is to partially fill the existing void of research concerning the divorce experience by providing a descriptive series of case studies of both working and middle class women's perception of that experience.

Statement of the Problem

The purpose of this study is to generate a description of the divorce experience from the perspectives of the working class and middle class woman and to investigate the relationship of socio-economic factors to post-divorce adjustment through a series of case studies. Insight into the following questions was sought:

1. How do the central themes develop out of the divorce experience among working and middle class women?
2. What differences and/or commonalities exist in the perceptions of the central themes between working and middle class women?
3. What relationship exists between post-divorce adjustment and the pre-divorce conditions of the marriage?
4. What differences and/or commonalities exist between working and middle class women's perceptions of their post-divorce adjustment?

2
Review of Related Literature

Central Themes in the Divorce Experience

The greater part of the literature on the divorce experience pertains primarily to the middle class; however, this literature is mostly speculative. These conjectures have not been substantiated through viable studies, but they do agree on general issues. One of the areas of agreement is the emergence of central themes among divorced women. These common themes are:

1. Intra-personal concerns regarding the emotional reaction to final separation;
2. Financial concerns;
3. Single parenting concerns;
4. Social concerns (dating, sexuality).

Further agreement exists among the sources of literature regarding the pre-divorce conditions associated with post-divorce adjustment. The pre-divorce conditions, it is thought, affect the development and resolution of the central themes. The pre-divorce conditions are the subject's perception of the following:

1. Pre-divorce experience of the marriage;
2. Inner strengths;
3. Support systems;
4. Familial relationships.

The present literature regarding central themes does not address itself to the differences between working and middle class experiences in the development of the central themes of divorce; however, there is extensive discussion of the middle class experience of divorce. This experience of divorce includes the central themes that follow.

6   Review of Related Literature

Emotional Reaction to the Final Separation

The reaction to final separation is described by several sources as a grief and mourning period. Kubler-Ross (1969) addresses herself to this period of mourning:

> This reaction happens with any loss, not just death. It happens if you are separated or divorced, or if you lose a boyfriend or a girlfriend. (p. 10)

Defazio and Klienboet (1975) refer to the behavior that accompanies final separation as part of a definite process,

> ...a process which at times seems an amalgamation of mourning and the infant separation from mother. (p. 106)

Waller (1930) concurs that:

> Like the bereaved one, the divorced has lost a mate...(p. 93)

The grieving process of divorce is marked by varying degrees of trauma (Goode, 1956; Weiss, 1975; Blumenthal, 1967). Goode's (1956) study indicates that the symptoms of memory loss, work inefficiency, poor health or poor sleeping are found among the divorced. He states that 50% of the divorced women in his study suffer from three out of four of these symptoms, indicating a high degree of trauma. Weiss (1975) reports two additional symptoms of trauma—anxiety attacks and loss of appetite.

In studies conducted by Goode (1956) and Toomin (1972), women describe themselves as progressing through the stages of numbness, denial, shock, rage, bitterness and depression. The findings of Hunt and Hunt (1977) concur with Toomin (1972), but include the feelings of guilt, shame, blaming spouse and a sense of failure. In addition, their study states that the depression following the final separation is punctuated with severe mood swings from relief and euphoria to suicidal tendencies.

Ernst and Loth (1952), Bohannon (1970) and Weiss (1975) add loneliness and panic to the list of emotional reactions. Krantzler (1976) describes early reactions to separation as:

> ...acute loneliness, self-pity, "emotional shakes and sweats", and a view of the future as a vortex of emptiness, fear, and uncertainty. (p. 45).

Women in Transition (1975) points out that the divorced woman experiences not only the previously-mentioned emotional reactions, but also a feeling of rejection that is difficult to overcome.

These emotional reactions are acutely felt during traditionally family-oriented occasions, such as holidays, weekends and nights. Yates (1976) states:

> You must be prepared to suffer through special occasions such as Christmas, birthdays, and your anniversary. These days bring a special kind of anguish. (p. 80)

Hunt and Hunt (1977) point out that loneliness is exaggerated by an empty bed at night and lack of shared activities for the weekend.

One of the major aspects of this emotional upheaval is the loss of identity. Weiss (1975) states:

> With the end of their marriage, most among the separated suffer the loss of some social scaffolding on which their self-definition had rested. (p. 94)

Waller (1930) addresses himself to this issue also:

> After any crisis which produces a really fundamental change in the conditions of life, the problem of re-integration becomes acute. The old self will not do: it has committed suicide by producing a change in the environment of which it was a function, the milieu in adaptation to which it was forged. (p. 103)

Fisher (1974) best summarizes this period:

> Divorce is the death of a marriage. With death comes mourning. With mourning comes feelings of relief, guilt, failure as a man or woman—either in bed or out, sadness and regret for what was and what might have been, rejection, loneliness, anxiety, hostility, depression. All the problems of self become exacerbated by divorce and mix with intolerable feelings of abandonment just when the concerns for a variety of practical problems of living loom large. (p. 186)

Financial Concerns

Even before the divorced woman begins to adjust emotionally, which may take six months to one year (Singer, 1975), women must begin to attend to the financial aspect of their lives. *Women in Transition* (1975) states:

> Women often find themselves with little or no financial resources and few marketable skills, while still others have professional status and have little difficulty adjusting. (p. 153)

Krantzler (1976) describes the results of the financial impact of divorce:

> Coping with a lower standard of living creates fear and, in many cases, humiliating and embarrassing living situations. (p. 40)

8   Review of Related Literature

Waller's (1930) study, although somewhat outdated, makes a specific statement about the difficulty of achieving financial stability in the case of women who do not receive alimony or inheritance:

> She must often take up some sort of occupation which will pay her an immediate salary and she has neither time nor money to invest in a long-term career. This shuts out many possibilities. More than likely she has been trained only for matrimony; matrimony is a specialized profession, and women who take that way of life must lose some of their adaptability. (p. 201)

In comparing the financial situation of divorced working class women and divorced middle class women, Weiss (1975) points out that in middle class professionally oriented situations, the economic problem may not be so great, but with low income families the struggle to maintain a household is difficult.

> The wife may be required to apply for public assistance. Application for public assistance... can be a humiliating experience. After filling out tedious forms and talking to several people, a process which takes hours, she must then ... be sent home to await a social-worker-investigator who must decide finally that she is genuinely impoverished.

In both cases, support payments, although one source of income, are often unreliable, making the financial picture unstable and anxiety producing (*Women in Transition,* 1975).

Hunt and Hunt (1977) state:

> The heaviest burden of coping (financially) falls on the mother who has been staying at home with her young children. Most of the time she must now look for work and this involves making day care or other arrangements for the children; it also means job-hunting, never the most pleasurable of tasks, and even less pleasant when harsh necessity creates an aura of desperation around the search. (p. 115)

Although the kinds of financial settlements divorced women receive and how the sum is arrived at is diverse, once the agreement has been reached the reality of everyday decisions becomes imminent. Such questions as where to live, how to live, how to get a job, what to do about children and how to do income tax returns are of paramount importance. The emotional turmoil involved with making these decisions becomes a major part of the trauma of divorce.

Single Parenting Concerns

Single parenting is often lonely and unmanageable. The custodial parent has total responsibility and may experience feelings of inadequacy. Abrams (1978) illustrates how these feelings can be compounded:

> It is hard for a woman to focus on her parenting role for the first two years after the divorce. Before that she is still in the "active bleeding" stage with many unresolved problems. (p. 54)

These feelings of inadequacy may lead to a super parent syndrome in which parents:

> ... try to be everything to the child: mother, father, teacher, etc. ... guilt feelings make her go through a period of trying to be Super Mom. (Abrams, 1978; p. 55)

In addition to feelings of inadequacy, single parents frequently have other kinds of fears (Abeel 1978 and Bennett 1978) such as:

1. Inability to make decisions;
2. Overwhelmed by responsibility;
3. Guilt at having caused the child to lose a parent;
4. Not being able to be both mother and father;
5. Conflicts between self interest and children's interest.

Kirsh (1978) speaks to still other problems of single parenting:

> ... there are all sorts of unexpected difficulties that are encountered, especially the first year. ... feelings of isolation, confusion about her new role, trying to organize her household and child-care chores. (p. 106)

Abrams (1978) mentions another phenomenon common to single parents, that of being the only single parent at family-oriented outings on the one hand, and the inappropriateness of bringing children to singles' functions on the other.

Still another area of concern for the single parent is trying to deal with the anger that children exhibit about the divorce which is generally directed toward the custodial parent (Weiss 1975). Weiss (1975) addresses himself to three other problems faced by single parents:

1. Discipline;
2. Aggravation cycle;
3. Unchallenged perceptions.

These three areas are related in regard to the sole responsibility aspect of single parenting. Children become difficult to manage with their own emotional turmoil over the divorce. The child challenges the parent's authority, the parent tries to maintain it, resulting in an aggravation cycle. Meanwhile, the single parent has no one to take over after her energy is depleted and no one to discuss childrearing practices with, thus, the unchallenged perceptions. Hunt and Hunt add:

> In addition to their struggles with guilt, single parents often find themselves in power struggles with their children. Many parents report a loss of governing power, when without a supportive co-parent on hand, she or he is cajoled or worn down by determined children. (p. 117)

In addition to child rearing, there are problems inherent in financially supporting the children. Working mothers mean baby sitters; baby sitters are an added expense, and they are unreliable (Yates, 1976). Abrams points out that if the cost of baby sitters is prohibitive, the child may be a "latchkey kid." Letting the child care for himself causes the parent to feel anxiety about his safety. Others viewing the situation of an unsupervised child may criticize the parent for being neglectful.

The parent's inability to find the time to resolve these fears and conflicts often leads to frustration which may result in an unconscious striking out at the children (Svary and Weston, 1978). However, no evidence indicates that single parents are more abusive than co-parents.

Establishing a social life is still another area of concern for single parents. Conflicts exist between personal time and family time. Questions about how much exposure new men should have to the children and vice versa, as well as how the new relationship will fit into the lives of her children and herself, and what can be expected in the way of relationship between the children and the man in the new relationship are all problems for the single parent (Mindley, 1969). However, as difficult as single parenting may seem, most women report that they prefer single parenting to being in an unsatisfactory marriage (Hunt and Hunt, 1977). In fact, the children may have a positive effect on the adjustment to divorce. Weiss (1975) reports that in many cases children provide structure to the mother's life and also that women often feel closer to their children when more of their energy is directed toward the children.

Social Concerns

Most people do socialize again after the divorce. In his book *The World of the Formerly Married,* Morton Hunt (1966) estimates that 75% of the divorced begin socializing the first year and 90% by the second year. (Weiss, 1977; and Krantzler, 1977) point out that when the divorced person starts to socialize again, he or she is faced with the conflict of wanting intimacy on the one hand and the insecurity of possible rejection and lack of knowledge of appropriate dating skills on the other. The newly-divorced find themselves with the dating skills reminiscent of their adolescent years (Hunt and Hunt, 1977; Krantzler, 1974). This conflict causes feelings of loneliness and desperation (Bohannon,

1968). The insecurity is heightened by the fear that they may be too old, unattractive, and if they have been rejected by the former husband, a feeling of worthlessness (*Women in Transition,* 1977).

There are two issues concerning sexuality which confront the divorced woman (Goode, 1930). The first issue is the need to reaffirm herself as a sexual being (Kessler, 1978), and the second is dealing with her children's negative reactions to a sexually active mother (Mindley, 1969).

When sexual activity begins again, it generally exceeds the level reached during marriage and is often accompanied by greater satisfaction (Goode, 1930; Bohannon, 1968). Sexual activity in the newly divorced is often an adventure in exploring the individual's potential sexuality. Napolitane and Pellegrino (1977) state:

> Most divorced women go through a Running Stage in which the choice of sexual partners may be pretty indiscriminate. But this stage doesn't last forever, and we usually learn about ourselves. (p. 83)

Some women state that they need to have many partners to re-affirm their femininity and build their egos after a bad marriage (Napolitane and Pellegrino, 1977). However, this exploratory phase is complicated by the prevailing attitude of society that divorced women are promiscuous and available (*Women's Survival Manual,* 1975). Subsequently, a conflict exists between the guilt associated with "should I?" and the loss of sexual satisfaction with "I shouldn't."

Along with the need for sexual reaffirmation comes the problem of a woman as a mother on the one hand and a sexually active person on the other. Cindy Mindley (1969) in her book *The Divorced Mother* discusses this issue:

> Condition your children in a relaxed way that you're going to date. Let them participate occasionally...do not include them in everything, or they'll get the idea your dates are actually theirs... The divorced childless woman is free to pursue any kind of love life she chooses. The divorced mother is not so free. (p. 201)

Mindley (1969), Napolitane and Pellegrino (1977) address the difficulties of deciding on the balance between children and sexual satisfaction. However, they do not offer any solution to the difficulties. They do concur that the need to be sexual is human. How much exposure the children have to the divorced woman's sexuality is an individual decision.

Resolutions of Central Themes

Over time, the resolutions of central themes result in the establishment of emotional adjustment manifested by a stronger ego identity, a growing sense of independence, stable family relationship and more social interactions. Resolutions of financial concerns are not included in even the most recent literature.

Singer (1975) considers divorce an opportunity for growth and development:

> Because people who divorce tend to remarry within a relatively short period of time, I shall herein consider divorce as the crisis point and post divorce and single life as an opportunity for further growth and development. (p. 116)

Weiss (1975) addresses himself to change:

> As decisions are reached and finally felt to be right, and as new decisions and new commitments are made that fit with them, the individual's life again assumes stable form. It becomes possible again to relate the present to the past and to see the present as moving consistently toward a desired future. The individual becomes once again the same person from day to day, just as was true before separation. Now, however, the individual is a different person from the one he or she was then. (p. 204)

Margaret Mead, in her article "Anomalies in American Post-divorce Relationships" in Bohannon's *Divorce and After* (1968) states that with the establishment of a stable family pattern, the difficulties inherent in single parenting decrease. According to Ann Barry (1975), increased emotional growth of the single parent results in a stable family pattern as evidenced by the dynamics of parent child interaction:

> The parents were clear about what kinds of rules and family help were appropriate and workable for them as individuals, and they had the cooperation of their children in maintaining their particular family pattern. (p. 302)

She continues in relation to the total growth potential of the single parent family:

> Perhaps the most significant quality these parents demonstrate is their own determination to succeed and their commitment to make their families as stable and nurturing as they possibly can within their own set of realistic limitations. Almost all parents in our research spoke of the personal growth they had experienced in the process of working toward this goal. Another outgrowth of such a commitment was the almost universal discovery that the well-being of the parent in charge of the family becomes an important basis for creating a sense of well-being in the family. (p. 303)

Much of the literature focuses on remarriage as an indication of satisfactory emotional adjustment. *Women in Transition* (1977), however, discusses several alternatives to remarriage. An intimate relationship may be living together partners, including both heterosexual and homosexual relationships, communal living or the option of the single life style.

Further, the development of an intimate relationship can be seen as a result of sexual growth. Hunt and Hunt (1977) state that:

> If the sexual behavior of the formerly married is hedonistic in intent, it is rehabilitative in effect. Through their casual and experimental sexual activity, females achieve more important goals than they sought. (p. 119)

The literature, although expansive in its coverage of the central themes of divorce, is lacking depth in studies concerning the resolutions of those themes. Furthermore, there are few studies regarding the process of the resolutions in post-divorce adjustment.

A Comparison Between the Working Class Marriage and the Middle Class Marriage

The literature reveals basic differences in the experience of marriage between the working and the middle classes, giving credence to the assumption that socio-economic factors may be a variable in the divorce experience as well. An examination of the differences between working class and middle class marriages will focus on the following areas:

1. Courtship;
2. Marital Roles;
3. Sexuality;
4. Child rearing.

Courtship

According to Rubin's (1976) study *Worlds of Pain,* the working class couple have generally met in high school and married shortly after graduation. Goode (1956) reports that they are usually engaged for three months. In contrast, the middle class couple, Udry (1966) reports, have met in college and generally marry sometime within two years of graduation. The engagement period, Goode (1956) states, is about a year. Current trends also indicate that many middle class couples are living together before marriage.

In the working class, the shortness of the courtship seems to be determined by two factors: (1) the woman is pregnant, or (2) both the man and the woman have a need to escape the controlling family situation. Komarovsky (1964) states:

> Marriage provides the most acceptable escape from an unhappy home. Moreover, marriage in itself is less restrictive because the working-class bridegroom enjoys some freedoms not granted the middle-class husband. (p. 325)

The working class adolescent, both male and female, is closely watched and controlled by the parents who fear that the child will become a delinquent. Further, unlike the middle class parent, the value systems of the working class parent do not accept alternative life styles or methods by which the young adult may enjoy the freedom of independence and sexual activity outside of marriage. In addition, the working class young adult has no fantasy beyond a "good job" and, therefore, considers marriage a natural rite of passage from adolescence into adulthood. (McKinley, 1964)

In contrast, the middle class, according to Rubin (1976) in her book *Worlds of Pain,* states:

> The young of that class find outside of marriage at least some of the independence and adult privileges that are available to the working-class young only within marriage. Thus, the children of the professional middle class consistently marry later. Among those I met, the average age at marriage was twenty-three for the women, and twenty-five for the men. (p. 96)

Furthermore, the choice of mate is closely scrutinized by middle class families according to Woods (1959):

> Marriage is subjected to family control to a greater extent than among other social classes... Sons who associate with girls from other social strata and consider marrying below their class status may be dissuaded by their kin. (p. 369)

Thus, the courtship stage for the working class is a natural progression of life and the growth process, while in the middle class, more thought goes into the mate selection process for reasons of class maintenance and personal growth. This is not to say that one class is more successful in its mate selection, or that one method is better than the other, but that motivation for marriage is perceived differently by the two classes.

Marital Roles

Rubin (1976) found that division of labor in the working class family is rigid. The husband is the provider, the decision maker and the final authority. The wife is not allowed to work and is expected to be housekeeper, cook and primary caregiver to the children. However, Rainwater and Handel (1969) found that in some cases:

> ...there is a shift away from a pattern of highly segregated conjugal roles and toward more mutual involvement between the two. (p. 115)

Hurvitz (1969) speculates that the situation of equality between husband and wife is an effect of the wife's demands for a change to more middle class values and this, in fact, puts an intolerable strain on the family.

In the middle class marriage Udry (1966) states that:

> The prevailing value in the middle-class families in the United States is that husband and wife decide most things together.

The husband and wife are both involved in the attaining of status in the career. She is the hostess for business meetings in the home. In fact, one of the motivations behind the middle class marriage is closely linked to career orientation according to McKinley (1964) in his book *Social Class and Family Life:*

> The home becomes a second office, where colleagues and business associates are entertained and business decisions are made... To some extent, the wife becomes a social and emotional assistant in the trials experienced by the husband in the work world.

In addition, McGinnis and Finnegan (1976) in their book *Open Family and Marriage* state:

> The domestic duties may fall to the wife, but if she is also career oriented, the domestic duties will be shared.

The roles in the middle class marriage are not rigidly defined. Kessler (1975) states that:

> the middle-class woman... manifests more confidence about her place in her husband's affection... these women appear to be less willing to sacrifice their own interests in order to please their husband.

Rainwater and Handel (1969) speculate that middle class husbands tend to be secure in their own identities as well. Consequently, the lack of role differentiation does not create as great a threat to either husband or wife.

In contrast, Hollingshead and Redlich (1958) point out that there are higher incidences of insecurity and lack of ego-identity among working class men. Hurvitz (1961) reasons that this lack of security requires that the working-class woman maintain her determined role so as to not increase the male's feelings of insignificance. It is important for the working class husband to be identified as the provider for his wife.

A comparison of marriage roles in these two classes indicates that working class marriages tend to be authoritarian with the husband at the head, while the middle class marriage tends to be egalitarian in nature.

Sexuality

McKinley (1964) hypothesizes that the division of sexual roles by the working class man is a direct result of class values regarding the physiological functions of the body. At an early age, working class children are expected to care for themselves, thereby losing the intimate physical contact between parent and child. The accompanying intimate emotional involvement of physical contact is not only lost but is taboo. McKinley further states that the lack of emotional intimacy from physical contact is transferred to the marriage. Sexuality becomes a physical relief for the husband does not necessarily include concern for the wife's enjoyment. Working class men try to satisfy their need for intimacy in erotic sexuality which is reserved for extramarital affairs sanctioned by the male peer group.

In her book, *The Blue Collar Marriage,* Kamarovsky (1964) states that women complain about the insensitivity of their husbands and tend to be unsatisfied sexually. She also points out that the women continue unsatisfactory sexual relationships because they experience some emotional intimacy which is not present in any other part of the marriage relationship. She also states that sexual adjustment or the lack of it does not affect marital happiness among the working class. McKinley's (1964) study hypothesizes about the reason for sexual relationships not having an effect on marital happiness. He reports that men rate their sexual role second after the provider role. The role of father is placed third. Women, on the other hand, rate their role as mother first, followed by homemaker, taking care of her husband and places the sexual role last.

In terms of sexuality, the middle class marriage continues to be egalitarian. Udry (1966) states:

> The common ideology developing in the middle class around this value is that men and women are basically equal in most of their intellectual, emotional and temperamental capacities, and especially in their sexual behavior. Men and women, then, have equal rights to the enjoyment of marital sex and should derive equal enjoyment from it. (p. 136)

He goes on to point out that middle class couples consider variety in sexual techniques and mutual satisfaction as a positive value.

Unlike working class couples who find sexuality outside of the engagement or marriage strongly discouraged by parents, the middle-class couple has no value around virginity or sexual monogamy. Hettlinger (1975) points out that the quality of the sexual relationship is of greater importance than sexual history for the middle class.

Greater opportunity for sexual experimentation is afforded the middle class through the college experience. Macklin, in her article "Going Very Steady" from *Readings in Human Sexuality* states that:

> Cohabitation is a widely accepted practice in most college environments, and it is seen as a natural part of a strong, affectionate but still tentative relationship... (p. 249)

The differences in attitudes between the two classes has its roots in early socialization. Children of middle class parents are educated about sex much earlier and with a more liberal attitude (McGinnis and Finnegan, 1976). This early liberal socialization is reflected in the less restricted adult sexual activities in the middle class. Komarovsky (1964) and Rubin (1976) state that guilt plays a role in the habits of the working class in sexual relationship, whereas in the middle class, loss of self-esteem is present when there appears to be no sexual opportunities.

Child Rearing

Parenting among the working class is described by Bronfenbrenner (1958) as a desperate attempt to control the behavior of the children so that they will exhibit traditionally middle class behavior patterns. He points out, however, that working class parents do not have the same economic leverage possessed by the middle class in enforcing the use of that behavior.

Komarovsky (1964) concurs that the middle class has greater financial and intellectual resources with which to control their children, while the lower class constantly stands vigil over their young to ensure control. This constant control, she points out, is exactly the impetus for the children wanting liberation and continually trying to get it by marrying young or by rebelling against all kinds of authority.

Furthermore, Rubin (1977) points out additional strain for the working class couple:

> Thus, like their parents, they believe that children need to be carefully and constantly watched... it was a sign of parental love and concern... Thus, both husbands and wives agree on the primacy of their parental responsibility... the demands of parenting often conflict with the needs of the parents for privacy, for shared adult time and leisure, for companionship, and for nurturance from a husband, a wife. (p. 103)

In the working class family, the wife is the primary care giver and has the most contact with the children. The husband sees his responsibility as making his children ready for the hard life they will have as adults. This divergency of parenting roles causes some conflict within the family as the wife thinks the husband is too strict, and the husband thinks the wife is too easy. The wife may even take the children's side against the husband, thereby disenfranchising the male.

In contrast, the emphasis in child rearing within the middle class is stated by Woods (1959):

> From babyhood to adolescence, the child is given time to learn gradually the highly abstract principles of status: his own position on the social ladder... (p. 83)

He goes on to point out that education is a value in itself and that 98% of the middle class children attend a pre-school.

Also, according to Udry (1966) in his book *The Social Context of Marriage:*

> ...American middle-class people increasingly have children "on purpose" by a deliberate decision to cease practicing contraception. (p. 10)

After making the decision to have children, many middle class couples then develop a library of books containing all the latest theories on child rearing. It is the middle class that becomes familiar with and puts into practice the most recent findings in child psychology. The raising of children then becomes an applied science. Cavan (1969) states:

> The impressing of habits and attitudes upon a child takes place primarily through the application of rewards and penalties. The middle-class parent tends to use rewards and psychological penalties which are more devastating to the personality than physical pain. (p. 47)

Even, a deliberate choice, children may cause strain on some middle class marriages by pulling the mother away from her career, changing the shared marital roles to more specialized ones, and by restricting the freedom of the husband's ability to take risks in his career.

The literature creates two distinct impressions of the working class and middle class in terms of child rearing. The working class family appears to accept parenthood as a natural extension of the marriage and to react from an emotional level when raising the children. Middle class parents, on the other hand, appear to take a less emotional, but highly regulated, view of parenthood.

In conclusion, Rubin (1976) specifies the differences between the working class and the middle class with the words if and when. The working class' attitude towards married life revolves around a tenuous if—if we buy a new car, if the children graduate, if I get a promotion. The middle class revolves around a solid when—when we buy a new car, when the children graduate, when I get a promotion. Most likely, the language differences will exist in the perceptions of divorce as well.

One interesting observation made during the course of the literature search is the difference between the amount of information that is available on the working class and middle class marriages. Several sources about the working class marriage were thorough and comprehensive. On the other hand, information about the middle class marriage was either combined with a discussion of several classes or found in very short discussions illustrating a particular point in a specific theory. There appeared to be no sources which were addressed solely to a comprehensive examination of the middle class marriage.

3
Methodology

Statement of the Problem

The purpose of this study is to generate a description of the divorce experience from perspectives of the working class divorced woman and the middle class divorced woman, and to investigate the relationship of socio-economic factors to post-divorce adjustment.

This study seeks insight into the following questions:

1. How do the central themes of divorce develop out of the divorce experience among working class women and middle class women?
2. What differences and/or commonalities exist in the perceptions of the central themes between working class women and middle class women?
3. What relationship exists between the post-divorce adjustment and the pre-divorce conditions of the marriage?
4. What differences and/or commonalities exist between the working and middle class women's perceptions of their post-divorce adjustment?

Definition of Terms

Working Class Woman—A woman who, with her former husband, fits the criteria of the social stratification category labeled as working class by level of education and occupation at the time of her marriage. (Broom and Selznick, 1960; Philips, 1979)

> Education: High school graduate or less
> Occupation: Skilled or semi-skilled labor, clerical work or retail sales.

(The women selected for this study are students at a community college and therefore constitute an exception to the traditional definition of the working class female. At the time of their marriage and divorce, they lived within the boundaries of traditional working value system.)

20   Methodology

Middle Class Woman—A woman who, with her former husband, fits the criteria of the social stratification category labeled as middle class by level of education and occupation at the time of her marriage. (Broom and Selznick, 1960; Phillips, 1979)

>   Education: Two years of college or more
>   Occupation: Professional, middle or high-level managerial positions.

Level of Involvement—Refers to the amount of time and emotional energy, either positive or negative, expended in the development of relationships within the pre-divorce conditions of the marriage.

Open-ended interview —An interview based on questions referring to a particular experience which elicits an unstructured response and permits the interviewer to investigate any aspect of the respondent's experience in depth.

Case Study—Thorough examination of a particular social setting and a detailed psychological description of persons in those settings. (Black and Champion, 1976)

Lived Experience—Whatever phenomena emerge within the individual's world that present themselves to her awareness. (Thines, 1977) This study will concentrate on the awareness about the specific event of divorce.

Central Theme—A recurring and/or unifying experience or concern common to the women interviewed in this study.

Inner Strengths—Internal resources directed toward the effective functioning or controlling of the outcome of one's own life.

Support Systems—Persons, groups of persons, and/or institutions that provide, through personal interaction, emotional support and external strength for the individual.

Research Method

The case study method using the open-ended interview was chosen as the data-gathering technique for this study. The use of this method promoted a clear, descriptive account of divorce as perceived by the two groups of women. In their book *Methods and Issues in Social Research,* Black and Champion (1976) quote Foreman (1948) in a discussion of the case study method:

>   ...a case study, basically, is a depiction either of a phase or the totality of relevant experience of some selected datum. (p.39)

In chapter 2, the literature referred to studies which relied on the survey or questionnaire type of data-gathering techniques. In some cases, the working class was mentioned but in most studies, the subjects were middle class. The survey method is a legitimate research method but has certain disadvantages that the case study method does not have. First, the questions used in the survey are determined by the researcher's preconceived idea about the experience; secondly, the survey reduces the experience to quantitative standardized units, thereby limiting the amount and scope of significant data that could be applied to an understanding of an experience.

Black and Champion (1976) state:

> A survey of the work done in an area... does not always produce the fresh, illuminating attack that a problem requires. Selective intellectual biases are usually more easily perpetuated than overcome. (p.73)

The case study method, on the other hand, is in its very character, qualitative and exploratory. Neale and Liebert (1973) state:

> The lack of control... permits things to "vary as they will," increasing the method's potential for revealing new and perhaps important findings. (p.68)

The case study method has another advantage in the proximity of the interviewer to the subject. This physical closeness allows the interviewer to observe the reactions of the participant to specific questions and further provides an indication of the intensity of that reaction. Under these conditions, an interviewer can use fundamental listening and observation skills to hear and see areas that need to be explored more fully. Rubin (1976) concurs:

> We have probability statistics on marriage, divorce, sexual behavior, and much, much more; but they tell us nothing of the flesh-and-blood women and men who make up the numbers. Therefore, we need... qualitative studies that can capture the fullness of experience, the richness of living. (p.25)

Komarovsky (1964) states in her book, *The Blue Collar Marriage:*

> The case study method was chosen for its advantage in conveying to the reader something of the flavor of the working class family life... Its job is to dissect, compare, abstract, and generalize, rather than to recreate the life of a group in its totality and uniqueness. (p. 26)

In summary, the case study method is specifically suited to this study for the following reason:

> The results of the past studies on divorce are statistically based and do not provide an in depth look at the experience from any single perspective. The case study method, on the other hand, provides an in depth exploratory view of the experience from an individual's perspective rather than from a group perspective.

Methodology

Subjects

The subjects for this study were twelve women, six of whom fit the definition of working class as outlined earlier and six who fit the definition for middle class as defined in the same section. In order to make the groups as homogenous as possible with the exception of class, all the women were Caucasian, between the ages of 27 and 33, had been divorced not less than one and one-half years or more than two years, had at least one child living with them and had been divorced only once. Caucasian women as subjects were chosen to limit the variable of cultural background as much as possible. The selection of women between the ages of 27 and 33 was based on the 1974 population statistics which indicate that the greater number of divorces occur within this age range.

Further, women with children were selected to provide information regarding the single parenting experience of the divorced mother. Women were chosen who had been divorced for not less than one-half nor more than two years for two reasons:

1. The women were able to easily recall the events and feelings at the time of the divorce; and
2. They had time to come to some resolutions concerning the central themes of divorce.

In keeping with the intent of the study which is to provide an in depth exploratory description of the divorce experience from two different perspectives, a group of twelve were chosen. It was thought that a larger number would prevent the opportunity for an in depth study and would destroy the exploratory nature of the study.

The following are biographical descriptions of subjects chosen for the study listed by class:

Working Class:

    Subject 1A—G—Age 33, married for 13 years, divorced 2 years, has 2 children, is a full-time student majoring in business administration.

    Subject 2A—B—Age 33, married for 14 years, divorced 1-1/2 years, has 2 children, is a part-time student majoring in secretarial science.

    Subject 3A—M—Age 31, married 9 years, divorced 2 years, has 2 children, is a part-time student in pre-nursing.

    Subject 4A—U—Age 27, married 5 years, divorced 2 years, has 1 child, is a part-time student majoring in secretarial science.

Subject 5A—J— Age 29, married 2 years, divorced 2 years, has 1 child, is a full-time student majoring in emergency medical training.

Subject 6A—T— Age 29, married 8 years, divorced 2 years, has 1 child, part-time student majoring in liberal arts.

Middle Class:

Subject 1B—G— Age 33, married 11 years, divorced 2 years, has 2 children, is a full-time college administrator.

Subject 2B—J— Age 33, married 10 years, divorced 1 year, has 2 children, is a full-time college instructor.

Subject 3B—T— Age 33, married 10 years, divorced 2 years, has 1 child, is a full-time college instructor.

Subject 4B—S— Age 29, married 4 years, divorced 2 years, has 1 child, is a full-time graduate student majoring in nursing.

Subject 5B—R—Age 32, married 9 years, divorced 1-1/2 years, has 2 children, is a full-time college instructor.

Subject 6B—E— Age 30, married 8 years, divorced 2 years, has 1 child, is a full-time para-legal.

Procedures

Population Selection

The working class women selected for this met the following qualifications:

1. They and their husbands, at the time of their marriage, were members of the working class as defined earlier.
2. Were between the ages of 27 and 33.
3. Were divorced for not less than 1-1/2 years and not more than 2 years.
4. Had custody of at least one child.

The working class women were students at the Community College of Allegheny County and volunteered to participate in the study after answering an advertisement in the student newspaper. Those women who responded to the advertisement were asked to fill out a biographical questionnaire (appendix B). Six of the women who met the qualifications, based on their answers to the questionnaire, were then contacted by phone and an appointment was made for the interview.

The middle class women selected for this study met the following qualifications:

1. They and their husbands, at the time of their marriage, were members of the middle class as defined earlier.
2. Were between the ages of 27 and 33.
3. Were divorced for not less than 1-1/2 years and not more than 2 years.
4. Had custody of at least one child.

The middle class women were referred by mutual friends. Following the referral, the women were contacted by phone and asked if they would like to participate. Those women who volunteered were then asked to complete the biographical data sheet over the phone. In turn, an appointment for the interview was made with those women who met the qualifications for the study.

Pilot Interviews

Two pilot interviews were conducted in order to refine the interviewing process, to promote the collection of significant data, and to enable the interviewer to conduct the interviews with ease. Those interviews were tape recorded and later analyzed to determine changes to be made in the process in order to acquire a clear in depth description of the subjects' experiences.

It was discovered, during the analysis of the tape recorded interview, that the structured interview originally designed for the study was too confining for the purposes of the study. The structured interview led the subject to respond methodically to the questions asked and promoted a description of events rather than experiences. For instance, the question, "What was your marriage like?" resulted in an answer describing a life style.

A new interview structure was designed using open-ended questions such as "Describe what it was like for you to be married." This type of question elicited answers which addressed themselves to the experience rather than the event. A question of this type was then followed by further queries designed to explore the experience in depth. It was found that the interview method using open-ended questions covered all of the areas needed for the study (pre-divorce experience of marriage, husband, children, in-laws, family of origin, the development of central themes and the resolution of central themes.)

Research Interview

The literature indicates that specific themes develop out of the divorce experience, that over time these themes become resolved through the process of post-divorce adjustment and that the pre-divorce experience of the marriage affects post-divorce adjustment. The interview was designed to explore the pre-divorce experience of the marriage, the emergence of the central themes of divorce, the resolutions of those themes in post-divorce adjustment and, in addition, any factors relating to the experience not discussed in the literature.

The interview began with an explanation of the purpose of the study—to generate a description of the divorce experience of women her age with custody of a child or children. The subjects were then asked to sign a voluntary participation document (see appendix B). The subjects were then told that the interview was to be taped for the purposes of being transcribed and analyzed at a later date, adding that during the interview it may be necessary to focus the responses on a particular issue in order to remain within the confines of the study.

The opening statements were followed by the question, "What was it like for you to be married?" or "Could you describe what it was like for you to be married?" After the answer to the initial query, questions were asked that were designed to expand the description, such as, "What do you mean by ...?" or "Could you give me an example of that?" Upon completion of the description of the marriage experience, the questions, "Could you describe how you felt at the time of the divorce?" and "What were you thinking about at the time of the divorce?" were asked. After the divorce experience was explored, the question, "How have things changed for you since the divorce?" was asked to begin the examination of the post-divorce adjustment.

When the subjects did not provide information concerning a specific area of the experience under examination, questions were asked that focused directly on that issue, such as, "What was your relation with your husband at that time?"

There were times during all of the interviews when the dialogue passed quickly from one issue to another. When that occurred, the subjects were either asked to go back and describe that particular part of the experience in more detail or the interview continued on with the flow of the experience without refocusing. It is felt, in those instances, that a refocusing would have reduced the clarity of experience being discussed. On still other occasions, subjects would begin to cry or their faces and voices indicated emotional involvement in the issue being discussed. On those occasions, the subjects were asked, "Can you describe how you are feeling now?" or "What does this mean to you?"

At the conclusion of the interview, an effort was made to allow the subjects an opportunity to address themselves to any issues or to make any comments that they wished.

Follow-up Interviews

It became apparent that important data was missing from the initial interview; thus follow-up interviews were conducted. The questions for this interview were specific and addressed themselves to the areas where information was lacking in each individual case.

Analysis of the Data

Each interview was transcribed and then read several times to gain an essence of the divorce experience for each subject. A summary of each subject's transcription was written. The summary included the biographical data gathered from the questionnaire administered prior to the interview.

Following the writing of the summaries, the transcribed interviews were read in order to extract descriptive statements concerning the subjects' perceptions of their divorce experience. For purposes of organization, the divorce experience was divided into three main areas which, in turn, were divided into categories to provide clarity. The three main areas and their subsequent categories were organized as follows:

The pre-divorce conditions:
1. Subject's perception of her marriage.
2. Subject's perception of her inner strengths.
3. Subject's perception of her support systems.
4. Subject's perception of her relationship with husband, children, in-laws and family of origin.
5. Other.

The central themes of the divorce:
1. Intra-personal concerns—emotional reaction to final separation.
2. Financial concerns.
3. Single parenting concerns.
4. Inter-personal concerns.
5. Other.

The resolution of themes in post-divorce adjustments:
1. Resolution of intra-personal concerns.
2. Resolution of financial concerns.
3. Resolution of single parenting concerns.
4. Resolution of inter-personal concerns.
5. Other.

The descriptive statements pertaining to each category were extracted from each interview one at a time so that each category was complete for each subject. The descriptive statements from each category for each subject were then placed on separate sheets by category and by subject. (appendix B)

It became apparent, at this stage in the analysis of data, that patterns were emerging whose scope and nature had not been anticipated earlier in the study.

One pattern concerned the issue of self-esteem and the questioning of self-worth. Middle class women questioned their feelings of self-worth early in the marriage, while working class women discussed self-esteem after the divorce. Descriptive statements concerning self-esteem were then extracted from the transcriptions.

The second pattern concerned the development of a central theme sometime after the divorce—that of establishing a new relationship with their ex-husbands. This theme was unresolved at the time of the interview. Descriptive statements concerning this issue were also extracted.

Limitations

1. The researcher was middle class and may have been biased from that point of view in terms of value orientations and language facility in the interviews with working class women.
2. Verbal limitation on the part of the interviewer may have inhibited sensitive communication of certain important issues.
3. Verbal limitation on the part of the subject may have inhibited clear description of the experience.
4. The gathering of significant data may have been limited by the researcher's and the subjects' ability to establish a rapport and trust.
5. The small sample used in this study for purposes of generating descriptive accounts was limited in its capacity to be specific.
6. Data was self report and, therfore, may have inhibited the subject in descriptions perceived as being socially unacceptable.

Delimitations

1. Women with children were subjects of this study.
2. Women who have not remarried were subjects of this study.
3. Caucasian women were the subjects of this study.
4. The study was confined to the event of divorce.
5. Populations from which subjects were selected were restricted.

4

Results

Design

A case study method utilizing an open-ended interview approach was used as the data gathering technique for this study. Twelve women were interviewed for one hour, focusing on the subjects' perceptions of their divorce experiences.

The interview focused on three areas of the divorce experience: (1) the pre-divorce experience of each subject's marriage, including relationships with husband, children, family of origin and in-laws; (2) the divorce, and (3) the post-divorce adjustment. Although the open-ended questions used in the interview (appendix B) focused on these areas, they were also designed to allow each subject to spontaneously and descriptively relate her individual perception of the divorce experience, as she perceived it. Biographical data questionnaires (appendix A) were also completed by each subject.

Subjects

Twelve divorced women, six of whom were working class and six of whom were middle class, participated in the study. Each woman had been divorced for no more than two years nor less than one and a half years. All had custody of at least one child. Each woman was Caucasian, between the ages of 27 and 33, and lived in the Pittsburgh area.

Five of the working class women were first semester, full-time students at the Community College of Allegheny County. One of the women was working as a secretary and attending school part time. The majors of the students varied. Two subjects were enrolled in transfer business programs, one was enrolled in the nursing program, and two were enrolled in career programs.

Each of the middle class women held at least a Bachelor's degree at the time of marriage. At the time of the interview, two were graduate students seeking a Ph.D. in nursing, three were instructors at local colleges and one was a para-legal. Five of the subjects had received their Master's degrees during the marriage, while one married shortly after receiving her graduate degree.

Data

The tape recorded interviews were transcribed. The transcriptions were read several times to gain a general impression of the divorce experience for each of the subjects. Each transcription was then read and analyzed to extract descriptive statements relating to the following three areas of the divorce experience:

The pre-divorce conditions:
1. Subject's perception of her marriage.
2. Subject's perception of her inner strengths.
3. Subject's perception of her support systems.
4. Subject's perception of her relationship with husband, children, in-laws and family of origin.

The central themes of the divorce:
1. Intra-personal concerns—emotional reaction to final separation.
2. Financial concerns.
3. Single parenting concerns.
4. Inter-personal concerns.

The resolution of themes in post-divorce adjustment:
1. Resolution of intra-personal concerns.
2. Resolution of financial concerns.
3. Resolution of single parenting concerns.
4. Resolution of inter-personal concerns.

The descriptive statements were placed on separate sheets labeled with each sub-division of the three main areas by subject. Significant data missing from the initial interviews were acquired through a tape recorded follow-up interview. This data was included on the descriptive statement sheets.(appendix C) The completed appendix C is on file with the Department of Counselor Education, School of Education, University of Pittsburgh.

After a review of the descriptive statements and the transcribed interviews, descriptive summaries were developed for each subject. The summaries were meant to convey a general sense of each subject's experience of divorce.

Descriptive Summaries

The following are descriptive summaries of the interview by subject. The descriptive summary is meant to convey the general sense of the open-ended interview.

Subject 1A—G

G is 33 years old. She was married at 18 and was divorced after 13 years of marriage. She has custody of her two sons, ages 10 and 12, is a full time student in a transfer business program.

G described herself as feeling lonely and rejected as a child because, "My parents were divorced; I was raised by my grandparents." G was sent to her grandparents because her mother had remarried an alcoholic who sexually abused her. G's perception of her mother is that, "She's a whiner and a complainer." G felt very close to her grandmother, however, and tried not to cause her any problems.

G became attracted to her husband because, "He represented the security of a stable family background," and he emodied all the traits that G felt were necessary for a happy marriage. She became pregnant and they were married. G's first disappointment with marriage concerned her husband's reluctance to tell his parents about the pregnancy. She said "He'd lie to me over and over again, just because he was afraid to tell them."

G felt that the incident with the early pregnancy helped to create a strained relationship with her husband's family. She said, "They assume that that was all me trying to keep it from them" (reference to pregnancy prior to marriage). G described her mother-in-law as needing a lot of attention, the responsibility of which fell to her. (Mother-in-law) "If she didn't get her way, she'd get migraine headaches. Then I was expected to call her every day."

Further disappointment came when G began to realize that her husband's closeness to his family was, she felt, a result of fear rather than love. She said, "I came to realize I don't think he really cared about them at all; I think he was just afraid."

After the initial disappointments early in the marriage, it began to go smoothly. As the marriage progressed, "I was happy, like all my dreams were coming true." They became involved in the church, bought a house, had two children, and were able to share the problems of her husband's developing career. G described her relationship with her children as not rewarding. She felt she had put herself in the background while promoting her husband's relationship with the children.

After a few years of marriage, G's husband began to abuse her sexually. She says of those times, "I was frightened. I felt depressed and isolated." G rationalized his behavior by attributing it to the stress of his job. G was resolved to keep her problem to herself so that she would not appear to be a failure and disappoint her grandparents. She would not give up her dream of a happy marriage and a secure family.

The marriage began to disintegrate when G discovered that her husband was having sexual relations with a friend of her sister's. She describes herself, "I felt sick, angry, and bad for all of us." She tried to convince her husband to go to a marriage counselor after the discovery, but he refused. They became separated at this time.

G recalls that year of separation as one of fatigue and emotional upheaval. She worried about the adjustment of her children. She thought about divorce, but became resolved to salvage the marriage and make it work so that her children could have a stable family, and she could have the security that she needed. During this year, G also got her first job and began to enjoy a sense of self-confidence.

G reconciled with her husband after this year of separation and describes herself, "I felt frightened and uncomfortable." She feared a continuation of the sexual abuse.

A few months after the reconciliation, G found out that her husband had propositioned her sister. She said, "I felt sick, disgusted, and disappointed. I felt sorry for myself and was feeling stupid for having put myself back in a position to be hurt again."

Once again, G tried to convince her husband to go to a marriage counselor and he refused. Again she felt isolated and alone, afraid to burden her family with her problems. She became depressed and asked, "What have I done to deserve this?" G began to have concern about her sanity and sought the professional help of a psychiatrist. The therapy lasted for three sessions, at which point she decided that she could not live in this situation any longer.

Upon making the decision to get a divorce, G recalls being frightened of the responsibilities of the children, as well as the financial and emotional decisions involved with raising them. She describes feeling happy when she went to work because she was able to remove herself from the situation for a short time.

After the divorce, G says, "I lived from day to day. I was busy all the time. I had no time to think about the future." Her family began to intrude on her life by giving her advice which she resented. G felt as if they did not trust her to handle her own life. She wanted to be independent and moved to Pittsburgh to insure that independence. She says of that move, "I was frightened and filled with fear of possible failure."

G states that she began to stop living day to day after the move to Pittsburgh. She stayed with a friend with whom she had been in close contact during the separation and divorce. G and her friend bought a house together. G was able to purchase the house after a financial settlement which gave her the proceeds from the sale of a house she and her husband owned jointly. In addition, she was able to go to school full time.

G says of herself, "I am pleased with myself. For the first time in my live, I'm important to me." She describes feeling good about herself and her ability to make decisions about her life and her children.

G's relationship to her children is a source of enjoyment for her now. She said, "I really love my kids. I take a lot of time with them." G says she is now the central person in their lives and enjoys raising them.

Subject 2A—L

L is 33 years old. She was married at 17 and was married for fourteen years during which two sons were born. At the time of the interview, her sons were 7 and 9 years old. L has custody of her sons, is working as a secretary and is a part time student.

L describes her family and marriage as being close. She attributes this closeness to an ability to communicate with her husband and he with her. However, this communication was based primarily on a traditional situation in which L and her husband accepted the traditional roles. She said, "He was the king, the lord, the master of the house. He was from the old school and so was I. We had open lines of communication." Although she could talk to her husband about experiences and share ideas, her husband made most of the decisions. In conjunction with the traditional roles, L described herself as a dependent person.

L's closeness in her marriage was reflected in her relationship with other members of the family. She was close to her children and participated in their lives. She said, "We did a lot of things together as a couple and with our children." She also pointed out that she took them and the marriage for granted. She appreciates them much more now.

L also had a very close relationship with her husband's family. She was a particular favorite of her mother-in-law. That close relationship has been partially maintained throughout the divorce and post-divorce period.

L's relationship with her family of origin was also close and points to that relationship as a source of strength during and after the divorce. She said, "My sisters and I have such a good time when we're together, and family gatherings are all the sisters, etc.," and "They (mother and father) gave me a lot of support through all of this."L explained that about half way through the marriage, she decided to brush up on her secretarial skills and get a job. Her husband's reaction to the schooling was negative and she felt that he was being counterproductive. After she had finished her courses, she went out to seek a job. She had some difficulty finding a job and was continually receiving negative comments from her husband.

L realized changes happening in her marriage when she finally got a job. She felt this job was a dream come true, and she did very well at it. The competence in her job began to build her self-confidence. She noted that with the newly found independence that her husband began to change his attitude towards her and put more pressure on her. She said, "His attitude was that if I wanted to work that was O.K., but I still had to do my other work."

Although L was aware of some changes in the marriage, she was unaware of any difficulties. She was completely surprised and shocked when her husband announced one morning that he had been having an affair and wanted a divorce. She speculated that the affair had occurred over a long period of time and that her husband had decided that she was now capable of taking care of herself. She stated, "The affair had been going on for some time, and they were just waiting for the time to be right. I guess when I reached the point that I did, it was now or never."

L recalled feeling shocked and disoriented. She felt that she had not fulfilled her role as wife and blamed herself. She said, "I felt devastated. I didn't feel at that point that I could possibly go on. I was really tearing myself apart inside and going over in my mind when I would go to bed at night—maybe I should have said that or maybe I should have handled that differently." During the first year after her husband left, she described being very unhappy, frightened and unable to organize her life. She described herself as feeling worthless and incapable of surviving on her own.

In addition to feelings of worthlessness and the emotional upheaval, L was concerned about finances. She felt overwhelmed with responsibility when she came to realize that everytime the car had trouble or something went wrong with the house, she would have to take care of it. She no longer had the security of having her husband see to the problems. Financial problems were compounded when she lost her job. She said, "But my emotional state was so bad at that point that the job that I had didn't last very long. I couldn't do my work so they let me go. That was a second blow."

L also became frightened of having the full responsibility of the children. She felt that her husband had abandoned the children and that this rejection caused emotional problems for her oldest son. She said, "But during that year (son) had a rough year in school. As a matter of fact, I had to work with the school nurse because he was emotionally unstable. He was having a lot of difficulty with the holidays and so was I."

L's difficulties with holidays and other family occasions were described as being the result of not feeling like a family without a husband. She explained that she did not trust men and did not start going out for about a year after the divorce. "I thought I'd never be able to trust another man. It took a long time to get over those feelings, too."

L discussed getting support and strength from two sources. The first source was external and came in the form of help from family and friends. Of her family, she said, "They gave me a lot of support (mother and father) I'd call my brothers-in-law; they would come out and help me. When I was down and out, I could call anyone (in the family) and they'd listen." She also got support from her friends. L stated that she was surprised at how much help they gave her and how many friends she had. She said, "I've always had a lot of friends but never realized how meaningful these relationships were with me until I was going through this crisis." L was able to find a new job several months after she was divorced and established new friendships which were also supportive. She said, "When I got this new job, there were a lot of people there who were in the same position I was in, and they gave me a lot of support.

The second source was internal. L explained that she was not a particularly religious person, but began to find comfort in prayer after the divorce. In addition, L began to realize that she was capable of managing her life well and that she was a much stronger person than she realized. Regarding her own inner strength, she said, "Then I became stronger with each month that went by. I kept getting stronger and inside it felt like I was building forces that I did not know existed."

During the post-divorce adjustment period, L explained that she began to build on these internal forces and began to change her outlook on her life and her situation. She said, "I learned that the world isn't going to stop and that life does go on. I didn't enjoy anything; then suddenly the seasons were having meaning for me, and I started to enjoy things again."

In conjunction with the decrease in emotional upheaval, L began to have more self-confidence. She stated, "It became easier and I became stronger. Each crisis that I went through gave me a feeling of self-satisfaction. That is solved, and I did it myself. With each crisis I said, 'Well, I've got a problem. How am I going to handle it?' I'd think about it and write myself notes. I really started to enjoy handling those things myself."

L says of herself now, "After a while, I decided that I wasn't the worthless person and that I could contribute something, and I still feel that I have not fulfilled my destiny yet. I had to overcome that first and find out what I was all about and then like myself."

She also described a fear of becoming too competent and too self-sufficient. L felt that she may not be attractive with her newly-found confidence. She said, "I worry about keeping my femininity. I've become more aggressive. I'm afraid people will be afraid of me."

At the time of the interview, L described the process of building a stable atmosphere for her children and establishing a better relationship with them. She said, "I think it took a full year of going through each season, going through the first Christmas, Thanksgiving and birthdays. I think I'm more understanding and more interested in their lives. I don't take them for granted."

L explained that her financial situation is still not completely satisfactory, but during the post-divorce period it became very difficult to manage because of her ex-husband. She explained the difficulties with, "He was sending money in the beginning and I was working, and so, financially, things were fine, but my emotional state was so bad at that point that the job I had didn't last very long. I couldn't do my work so they let me go. I got unemployment and I went down to try to get food stamps. They looked at my budget and decided they didn't know how I was doing it, but because I had a house and a cottage, I wasn't eligible. His leverage over me to force me to give him the divorce was the money, and he completely withdrew that from me for awhile." At the end of the interview, L had gotten a job that she was happy with and was able to get a second part-time job. She explained that, "Financially, I still have rough spots, " and "Sometimes I get tired, but I feel good about having the skill to get a job and hold it."

Socially, L eventually started to go to singles bars with friends. She explained that at first she had great difficulty with dating again. At the time of the interview, however, she had a stable intimate relationship which she described with, "I'm dating a very nice man and have fallen deeply in love with him. I'd like to marry someday, but not now. The ideal situation would be to live with my friend."

L discussed still having some difficulty understanding the divorce and regretted the lack of a relationship with her ex-husband. She said, "He doesn't even see them (children). He completely turned his back on me. I actually feel sorry for him."

Subject 3A—M

M is 31 years old and has been divorced two years after nine years of marriage. During the marriage, a son and a daughter were born. M has custody of both children, ages 8 and 10. M's marriage was described as being good in the sense that she, her husband and her children used to do a lot of things together as a family and that she and her husband could communicate well.

M explained that, as part of his military assignment, her husband was stationed in Georgia. During the assignment, the marriage began to show signs of strain. M related that money became a problem due to the high cost of utilities. In addition to the utilities, her son became sick often causing more financial strain.

In conjunction with the financial strain, she felt that the visits by relatives put an added burden on the relationship by reducing the amount of time she and her husband spent together. "We had a lot of company in the summer. That can put a lot of strain on the marriage."

During the marriage, M's relationship to her husband was traditional in that he was the provider and she took care of the domestic duties. M expressed resentment over the responsibility she had at that time with, "I did everything." She also expressed resentment with her husband's inability to accept her opinions as being valid. She said, "Even though we could talk, he always had to be right."

Even though she expressed resentment, M felt that she had been a good wife and mother. She also felt that she had shouldered a large portion of the responsibility of the marriage and saw herself as being independent. She said, "I guess before the divorce, during all that time that I was married, I carried all the responsibility."

Toward the end of the marriage, M became aware of her husband's seeing another woman. She attributed his infidelity to the financial difficulties in the marriage with, "He just couldn't handle it." M described her reaction to her discovery with, "I cried all the time. I was just nervous and panic-stricken."

In addition to the emotional reaction, M found herself without money to feed the children. She said, "I didn't know where in the heck the food was going to come from for the kids. There was no money. He decided that he would hold the money, so he held the money."

In an attempt to save the marriage, M suggested that she and her husband seek marriage counseling. Her husband refused and told her that he wanted a divorce. At that time, M explained that the problems began to mount for her and she lashed out at her children. She said, "When I had all these problems build up on me, things were really bad. I used to take a lot of my problems out on my kids. I used to beat them. I mean I beat them a lot."

M was able to feed her children and get emotional support for herself initially by going to neighbors. She stated, "My girlfriend—she's really all I had. I'd go down to my girl friend's house and she'd feed the kids," and "I mean I had my neighbors, my friends. They'd give me advice, and if I went and cried on their shoulders, they'd be there."

Eventually, M decided that she would have to take some action to improve her situation. She said, "I was still panicked, but I knew that things weren't going to get any better by staying there, and I had no one to help me so the only person I could turn to was her. So I called my mother and she sent me the money and I left." M came back to Pittsburgh and lived with her parents for a short time. She said of her family's support, "We were always close, but during that time we lived out of state for a long time. I had to decide what was right for me." M was in contact with her in-laws also who gave her some support. She said, "He doesn't have much of a family. He has only two sisters and his mother is dead. I have contact with one sister. She just can't accept what he did, and she can't accept his new wife."

M, although living in Pittsburgh and separated from her husband, did not want the marriage to end. "I really didn't want the marriage to end. I didn't want it. I didn't want the divorce. I wanted to see a marriage counselor, at least to try and see if we couldn't work it out."

M described feeling disappointed and devastated over the impending divorce. She described feeling hopeless in terms of her competing with her husband's girlfriend with, "I mean she was skinny and young and pretty. I couldn't compete with her."

After returning to Pittsburgh, M had no money. She lived with her parents for awhile and then applied for welfare and low-income housing. "After I got home, I made an appointment with welfare. I went looking for low income housing and then after that I filed for support. Welfare is like no money at all."

In addition to the financial problems, M was concerned about emotional problems her children were displaying. Her daughter began to stutter and her son began to misbehave in school and have speech problems also. She said of this time, "I beat them a lot. I felt bad. And my daughter, she was a nervous wreck. Then when I found out that my son had all kinds of speech problems, I had to have therapy for him. He was really bad." The school recommended a speech therapist for her daughter. The therapist recommended that M see a social worker. Of the experience with the social worker, M said, "Talking to that lady (social worker) calmed me down, and I haven't touched them since then, and I'll tell you that really upset me too. Thank God that help was there."

M's social life, just after the divorce, consisted of going to singles bars with her sister. She found the combination of her family responsibility and dating difficult to manage. She stated, "It's hard going to school and taking care of the house and taking care of the kids and all the things you have to do when you're single." She became disillusioned with dating saying, "Men only want one thing and that's not for me. So I quit. There just wasn't any social life."

The divorce became final about a year after M moved to Pittsburgh. She didn't want the divorce and resented the easy way with which the divorce was obtained. She said, "Maybe it could have worked out if it (getting a divorce) were harder."

At the time of the interview, M, with the help of a social worker, had begun to accept the divorce. She said, "She offered pointers and it helped me sort out my feelings. I started to get in touch with myself and not think about the divorce so much." In order to help herself, M has kept busy with school and other activities. "I keep busy all the time. I go to school, I visit my sisters, volunteer at the Head Start Center, and I sell Tupperware sometimes. Anything I can do." She says of her life now, "I started to pick the pieces up and now it's almost together."

M feels better about herself and attributes her sense of well-being to better adjustment on the part of her children. She stated, "I'm more at ease with myself now and they're better for it." She said of her children, "They have really adjusted well. (Daughter) especially doesn't get upset the way she used to. My son is just like a normal boy."

M's concern about her children, at the time of the interview, was primarily financial. She said, "As far as food and clothes go, I get a lot of help from my family, but to come up with some extra money to go to Kennywood or to the movies or MacDonald's. The things you want to give your kids and you can't."

Between the time of the divorce, M made a decision to return to school in order to get the skills necessary to support her children and herself. She said, "I figured that with some kind of trade or nursing, I could get a job and go back South. It's too cold up here." M fantasized about finishing school with, "When I get out of school and get out and get that job and just have my own home and a car and see that my children have what they want to have, well, that's it. That's what I'm working for."

M was beginning to adjust to being single although she would like to marry again. She stated, "I'm discovering that it's not so bad being single. I feel good about it, but I can't say it's the best life. I'd like to get married again." However, M has still not started to date again.

M expressed excitement about having discovered herself and her abilities with "I'm branching out to do other things, and I'm discovering more of who I am and what I can do than what I was." She did, however, express difficulty establishing a new relationship with her ex-husband who has remarried. "We don't get along at all. I would like to see us straighten out some of this." M discussed what might have happened if she had contested the divorce with, "Sometimes I wonder if I had contested the divorce would it have made things better. Would he have given the marriage a second chance." M also talked about moving closer to her ex-husband after she graduates. She said, "After I graduate, I could move where he is so that the kids could have more of a father."

Subject 4A—U

U is 27 years old, and, at the time of the interview, had been divorced for two years after five years of marriage. During the marriage, a son was born. U has custody of her son who was 4 years old at the time of the interview. U is now enrolled in a career program in secretarial science at Community College of Allegheny County.

U described her family as being close in the sense that she was loved and given guidance as a child. However, she felt some resentment toward her parents for not preparing her for the difficulties of her marriage. She stated, "My parents never fought or had an argument. I got to think that marriage was like smooth sailing so that when it happened to me the way it did, I was just unprepared."

U explained that her marriage was similar to that of her parents in the beginning in that it ran smoothly for a while. She married while her husband was in the military. They were not living together for the first eight months of the marriage, but she joined her husband at his duty station at the end of that period. She and her husband lived in a house with six other military men. She said of this situation, "It was an odd situation in that it was all guys and one female in that house."

U worked while they were living in Maryland and eventually became pregnant. She explained that the marriage "was working out fine" until the baby was born. She said, "After the baby was born, he started to take drugs and then the beatings started." From U's description, it is apparent that the baby, although it may have been related to his behavior, was not the main cause. She explained, "There was this scene where he told me he fell in love with another woman. Things just kind of blew up then. I started bugging him. I guess I looked like an eyesore or something."

During the period after the baby was born, U recalled feeling rejected, humiliated and fearful. Her fear was based on feelings that in her absence her husband might strike out at her son. She said, "I was working about 4 or 5 hours at night, and I was always afraid of what might happen if (husband) got mad at (son) for something, would he clobber the kid." U felt it was necessary for her to work in order to buy food and gas for the car. She explained that the rest of the money went for drugs.

U described herself as not being an affectionate person towards her son. She said, "As far as affection goes, it's hard for me to give it to my son." She had been abusive towards her son during the marriage. She said, "I have put black and blue marks on him and that scared me because I think I'm abusing my child." She feared that her son's watching her being beaten might have had a negative effect on him. U also fears that by using his father as a model he may also become abusive. She stated, "I don't want him to do to someone else what his father did to me," and "If it kills me, he won't be like his father."

Eventually, U left her husband for a short time. She felt that she was unable to handle the problems of mounting bills, repeated beatings and feelings of inadequacy. She said of this time, "After the beatings, he was irresponsible and wouldn't pay bills. I just couldn't take any more of the beatings." U wanted to try and keep the marriage in tact so she returned five days after she left. She said, "I left after Christmas for five days. I came back again and tried to give it a second chance. That didn't work out for about four months. So we agreed on a divorce." Of herself, U said, "It destroyed me emotionally and I left."

At the time of the final separation, U recalled feeling angry and rejected. She said, "I couldn't take it any more. It was just a losing battle." U recalls blaming herself for the break-up of the marriage and had a lack of confidence in herself.

U went to live with her parents in Ohio. She credits them with helping her recover from the emotional upheaval of the separation and divorce. She said, "I think my parents helped me through part of the feelings of anger and rejection during those months.

U's financial concerns occurred in conjunction with her single parenting concerns. She said she, "knew I could always get a job," and she saw that as one of her strengths. However, she wasn't sure she could support her son and give him what he needed as well. She said, "My first fear was was I going to be able to give him the things that are basic for a child. I questioned like am I going to be able to keep (son) fed and will I still be able to do the things I want to do." U was able to get a job shortly after moving to Ohio. She continued to live with her parents.

U felt that as a result of the beatings and verbal abuse she received during the marriage, she was unable to feel comfortable socializing directly after the divorce. She said, "I was shy and had to be drawn out in the office," and "It was a direct result of the marriage, the beatings and the put-downs."

A few months after the divorce, U's mother-in-law visited her grandson in Ohio and offered to take custody of her grandson while U went back to school. She said, "She (grandmother) made me an offer to take (son) off of my hands for a year while I went to school in Ohio." U's relationship to her in-laws was explained with, "I have a lot of respect for her and Dad, and I do love them like I love my own parents." She decided to accompany her ex-mother-in-law and her son to Pittsburgh and live with them.

U claimed that she was unaware that her ex-husband was living in the house at the time, but her motivation for returning was explained with, "I'm staying there just to be an irritation to him. I see it as a golden opportunity to give back what he gave me."

Because of this living arrangement and the antagonism between U and her husband, several problems have arisen with their son which concerns U. She said, "He wasn't that aggressive when we first came here. He seemed to be a good little boy. He'll say no to them (grandparents) and he'll smack me. For no reason he goes up and smacks people." U feels that, "He seems to lack attention and this is the way he gets it. So I feel I have to get out of the house and pay more attention to him in my own apartment."

U also complained about becoming nervous again. She said, "I'm nervous most of the time. I don't know when it's going to come," referring to verbal attacks by her ex-husband. However, U stated that she felt more confident about her ability to be successful as a provider.

At the time of the interview, U was involved in a stable relationship, but still has reservations about making any relationship intimate and/or permanent. She said, "I still don't trust men. I sort of look at them as sheep in wolves' clothing. There's always that little catch that says don't do it, at least not now."

U was also looking for an apartment but was having difficulty finding one that would accept children that she could afford.

Subject 5A—J

J was 29 years old at the time of the interview, had been divorced for two years and had custody of her daughter, age 2. She is now enrolled in a career program in allied health at the Community College of Allegheny County.

J was married at 25 while she and her husband were in the military. J says of her relationship with her husband, "I was more in love with love than with my husband." She knew her husband 18 months before they were married, and she says of that time, "I don't know why I married him because I knew he was going to Turkey, but I thought he'd take me with him."

After her husband's return from Turkey, J noticed a change in his attitude toward her. She describes this change, "He was getting like you do what I say or else." Further strain was put on the marriage with a move to Georgia: "He came back and we went right to Georgia. It was strange because I didn't know anybody, and it was so hot, and I was homesick."

While in Georgia, J became pregnant. She says of the pregnancy, "He said he really wanted to be a father, and he really wanted me to get pregnant, but then at the last minute he was going to chicken out and there was nothing I would or could do." J described her husband's position about the pregnancy, "He said we can't afford this child because he was $10,000 in debt. So he said either you get an abortion or put it up for adoption, but we can't raise it together." In addition to the conflict over the pregnancy, J describes other problems in her relationship with her husband, "The fact that he was drunk almost every night. I didn't know if he was going to hit me or what he was going to do." J also felt left out of the decision making in the family, "He didn't consult me about anything." J also remembered her husband humiliating her in public, "He had debts everywhere and then he'd go into Sears and say she doesn't need a credit card because she doesn't act like an adult."

J discussed her attempts to maintain the marriage: "I thought raising a child in this day and age was going to be a pretty hard thing to do without a father." She said, "I was thinking we should go to a marriage counselor, but I couldn't find any." J described her husband's reaction to counseling, "The words just poured out of his mouth when he got drunk, then he'd be sorry for it the next day and I said to him, 'Look, you gotta go (to counseling), and he said, 'No, I'm not going to go. It's all your fault."

J's decision to separate from her husband was based on the difficulty over the pregnancy and his refusal to go to a counselor, "I said if you're not going to go then I'm going to go, and I packed my stuff and left."

J expressed fear as a reaction to the separation. She said, "I was more scared at being pregnant. I was five months pregnant and I had toxemia. Going to a new O.B. was scary and there are so many in Pittsburgh."

J's daughter was born five months into the separation. She decided to keep her daughter after the delivery. "It took me until then to decide. I had a big decision to make about if I should keep her or put her up for adoption, and I decided to keep her."

J's husband filed for divorce during this separation. She describes her reaction to the filing saying, "I was angry. When I got served with the papers, I thought screw you. O.K., you can have it."

J described herself as getting strength from three sources during the difficult times in her marriage and then with the divorce. She said, "The thing I saw most is that I wanted (daughter). I couldn't see going and getting pregnant and giving her up for adoption." She also said of herself, "I think I'm stubborn. You know not to let it get to me." In addition to the stubborness, J described another defense, "I think I put up a shield and I wasn't about to let it down. I can protect myself that way."

J said she also got support from two friends. She said of one friend, "I'd call her on the phone and I'd tell her the things, and she just said, 'Hang in there. It's going to be over with soon.' I sort of listened to her because she knew what she was talking about." She described her friends helping her when she separated from her husband by keeping her occupied, "Taking me out every night and just keeping my mind off the problem."

J described her relationship with her in-laws as both good and bad. She said she didn't have too much to do with her husband's father and his mother was dead, but she had contact with his sister. She said of the family, "They were no problem. They were happy he'd found somebody he liked and could settle down with, but I don't think they knew what he was really like."

J's relationship with her family is strained. She says of her mother, "My mother was and is real protestive." J did not refer to her father, but said of the relationship with her mother, "One simple word. Like hell. It was not a real good relationship and not even now."

J lived with her mother through the separation and divorce. She said of that time, "She had a housekeeper. She gave me lists of things to do every day." At the time of the interview, J was still living with her mother and repeatedly expressed her need to get a job and be able to support herself and her daughter. Living with her mother was part of a solution to the lack of finances for J. She was not sure her husband would support her child.

After the baby was born, her husband paid child support after J sued him, "After I took him to court, he upped it to $156 a month (child support). In addition to child support, J found it necessary to get more financial aid through welfare. She recalled the experience as being humiliating with, "I don't like going down there in the first place and then going down and fight with those people in the welfare office." J was also able to obtain grants in order to go back to school and gain skills as a para-medic.

The initial single parenting concern for J was whether or not she would keep her baby. She decided to keep her after doing some reading about single parenting. She said, "I read a lot about single parents, and I figured if they could do it then I could too." She recalled that when she brought the baby home from the hospital, she had no one to help her and she felt tired all the time. It was a difficult time and she did not enjoy the baby. She said, "I didn't have time to enjoy her because people were telling me what to do."

J enjoys her child now and finds her biggest problem is finding adequate child care. She said, "As hard as its been, it gets easier. I like raising her now." She is looking forward to graduating so that she and her daughter can move to their own apartment.

Of her social life, J explained that when she was first separated, "You felt funny being single and pregnant, so I just stayed home. I had no social life." However, in the beginning, she enjoyed being single, but she said, "As time went on, I didn't think it was so great (being single). It was hard." J felt it as hard in the sense that she was still dependent on her mother. At the time of the interview, J was not dating but she expressed a desire to marry again with, "Oh, yeah. If I could find somebody to do it (get married again)."

J's relationship with her ex-husband is described as, "So my relationship with him is strained again." This strain is the result of her husband writing her a letter asking her if she wanted to get back together. She had ambivalent feelings about a reconciliation which surfaced when he came to visit shortly after the letter. She said of that meeting, "I was a little joyed at seeing him, but I wasn't overly thrilled. There was no discussion of going back together. I was relieved." She said of his leaving that day, "I was sorry to see him go."

At the conclusion of the interview, she was not absolutely sure that she did not want to see her ex-husband again, but felt that a reconciliation would probably not happen. She again expressed the desire to graduate and be on her own.

Subject 6A—T

T is 29 years old. She married at 19 and had been married for eight years before her divorce. T has been divorced for two years. She has custody of her eight year old daughter. T had graduated from high school, but her husband had not finished high school.

T described a family situation in which her mother gave her the responsibility of taking care of her brothers and sisters. She said, "My mother is mentally ill and has been for years. I have two sisters and a brother who were in my care since I was fourteen." Of her father, she said, "My father, he on the other hand, is in his own little world. Everything goes right." She added, "I hate to talk about them; they are both so good."

T got married in order to get away from her family and another boyfriend. During the marriage, T was sexually abused and felt that her husband wanted to maintain complete control over her life. She said, "Sexually, he made my life a nightmare. Just day and night and day and night and after me sexually all the time," and "Well, he followed me around all the time. He'd call me 10-15 times a day."

T explained that her husband's attitude towards her was a result of his family background. "He never knew he was doing anything to me. It was 'You're my wife and you do what I say.' He was brought up that way." She felt that she was more intelligent than he was and came from a higher socio-economic group.

T recalls that her mother-in-law hated her, but that her father-in-law often protected her in family disturbances. She stated, "His mother hated me. Two months after we were married she started a big fight. She hit me and started screaming and then she hit me and I hit her. His father started after me and I ran out of the house. When he caught up with me, he asked me what was going on. He ended up being the best friend I had in that family."

During the marriage, T's husband would not allow her to have any friends. The people they socialized with were his friends whom she described as "weirdos." T became unhappy and put on a lot of weight. She also became sickly and was in the hospital several times. She said, "He had me so mentally upset... I had doctors who told me to leave."

A daughter was born a few years into the marriage. Two weeks after the delivery, T's husband insisted that she go back to work. She said, "I was in no condition. I weighed 200 pounds and I was depressed." While I was working, the baby was in a day care center and in the evening she would hire a baby sitter so that she and her husband could go out. She said, "I never saw her, but when I did I enjoyed her." When asked how she felt about her daughter, she said, "I couldn't feel about anything when I was married to him" T credits the absence of time with her daughter for helping her make the decision to leave. She said, "(I felt) very unhappy. That had a lot to do with my decision."

Further credit for the decision was given to friends she made on her new job. She said, "They encouraged me before I had any idea that I was going to leave." One friend offered to let T stay with her if she decided to leave. Before the suggestions from her friends, T explained that she had no thought of leaving because, "I had become adjusted to what I was living with."

T eventually lost the job she had gotten after the baby was born because her husband told her boss she was quitting. She managed to get another job which paid her enough money so that she could support herself and her daughter. It was at that point she left.

T felt embarrassed about the separation and divorce and was concerned about what her family would say. To her surprise, both her parents gave her support. "He (father) was behind me all the way. My mother was behind me all the way too."

After leaving her husband, T was relieved and happy to be out of the marriage. She stated simply, "I was exalted." However, she was concerned about the responsibility of taking care of her child by herself and frightened about what she thought her husband would do in retaliation. Because of the lack of financial difficulties, T's main concern was about her child and her ability to be a good parent. She said of her daughter, "She was emotionally upset. I felt sorry for her."

T began to feel overwhelmed by the responsibility of her daughter and said, "I needed a break. It's not a break from the kid. It's a break from the responsibilities."

Much of T's relaxing came in the form of going to singles bars with her friends. She described her dating pattern as one she believed was satisfying because other people had told her so. She said, "I believed everything that was going around. I went to singles bars and I got picked up." However, she quickly became disillusioned with the bar scene and said, "You finally decide you're not going to do it just because you don't want to do it. Then you can establish some kind of peace of mind for yourself." T felt that her peace of mind came from her starting to make active decisions about her life and how it was going to be.

T was starting to make those decisions when her husband initiated the first of several custody suits against her. She said of that time, "They straightened out real fast when I had the first custody hearing. I did nothing but sit down and figure out how I was going to be perfect. As part of the decision making process, T and her daughter were in therapy for a year following the separation.

Regarding her daughter, T decided that she would provide all the care for her child and that she would not give that responsibility to baby sitters: "I would send her off to school and I would be the one waiting for her when she got home. I would make her dinner and put her to bed." T was able to afford the time for being the primary care giver because of the lack of a job and financial difficulties which happened after the divorce.

Although she had a job at the time of the separation, her husband continued to harrass her on the job, and she eventually was fired. She got another job, but lost that after he began coming there and disturbing her. She explained that she got a part time job then and got partial welfare. Again her husband harrassed her. She said of this time, "Then I got to the point where everything I would do he'd take away from me and finally I went half on welfare. I was so put down. I just gave up. I'll just go right down to the bottom and then you won't have to push." Her husband had been providing her with child support from the time of the separation. She said of her financial situation at the time of the interview, "Financially, I'm a disaster. That's my situation now. Welfare and child support."

During the time between the divorce and the interview, T had resigned herself to not having a relationship with a man. Following the disappointment of the singles bars, however, she became involved with two men. Of the first she said, "Emotionally he didn't tax me. I had a good sex life and a good friendship." T attributes the end of that relationship with trouble with her ex-husband. Of the second and present relationship she says, "This is the first time I have ever been in love. He doesn't keep holds on me. He doesn't put me down or try to possess me."

T's relationship with her ex-husband at the time of the interview was described as, "Very shaky. Very, very shaky." She feared that he would continue to harrass her and said she was nervous about him most of the time. She said, "I feel like everytime I aggravate him I'm going to get it." The relationship with her ex-husband is seen by T as a determining factor in how she sees herself. She said, "I'd be fine if I could just get over the feeling that he (ex-husband) was going to do something to me." However, she felt that she is beginning to see positive aspects in herself. She said, "I'm branching out to do other things and I'm discovering more of who I am and what I can do than what I was."

Subject 1B—G

G is 33 years old. She was married at the age of 20, after completing two years of college to a man who had recently completed graduate school. After eleven years of marriage, during which time two children were born, G and her husband divorced following a two year separation. G and her ex-husband live within several blocks of each other and share custody of their two children. Her sons are ages 9 and 11.

G left college to marry a man she had known for two years. She had had a relationship with another man who she said she felt very good with and thought was very special, but her parents did not approve of him. Her parents approved of her husband and thought he was a good catch. He was a college graduate and was about to go into graduate school when they married.

G described her parents as being demanding and not accepting of her as she is. She sees her family now as being supportive, and as loving her, but still not accepting. She stated, "I guess the positive parts of it are that I know they love me, and they are supportive of me right now, but they saw me as a sixteen year old even when I was no longer sixteen, and expecting me to merge with their values, and that was a major difference between (husband's) family and my own. They have accepted differences in values; my family has not." On the other hand, G's discussion of her in-laws reflects her perception of mutual love and respect. She said of her in-laws, "Everybody treated me very warmly."

She still maintains a close relationship with her ex-husband's family. She said, "I spent a vacation with one of his brothers about a year and a half ago and just enjoyed myself a lot."

Shortly after the marriage, G and her husband moved to Pittsburgh where her husband was in graduate school. She says of the marriage, "We became closer then because we were the only people we knew." G worked and finished her Bachelor's degree while her husband was in graduate school.

G described her perception of her marriage in ambivalent terms. She stated that, "Well, parts of it were good and parts of it were not so good." G discussed the good times as those during which her husband was supportive of her and they became very close. She said of those times, "It was a caring relationship," and "We had similar tastes in a lot of things and began enjoying doing things together. It was almost like a merging." G discussed the bad times in the relationship as her husband being critical of her and, at the same time, perceiving him as being very sure of himself. She remembered that her husband used to "pick at me constantly," and "I remember times he'd throw food on the floor and I'd go and clean it up and I took it." You see there wasn't anything that I could do that he couldn't do better. She also expressed that she felt like a burden to her husband with, "I never made a decision. He had to make them, and you can imagine what a burden that must have been for him to have someone who just wouldn't make a decision. I made it up to him by never saying no."

48   Results

After G's husband finished graduate school, he accepted a job in Pittsburgh, and she felt more permanent. G got pregnant and had a son. She describes herself as "exhausted much of the time, and I got no relief care from him." Her husband had not wanted the baby at that time. He told her it was her full responsibility. G spent much of her time trying to fit into the role of wife and mother but felt that her husband did not approve of her ability to parent.

G's experience of parenting and her relationship to her children during the marriage was one of disillusionment, disappointment and feelings of inadequacy. In reference to disillusionment and disappointment, she said, "I expected that when I had kids that everything would be sweetness and light. That was an illusion. When I found out how much work it was, I felt inundated by the work and not really excited except they were so pretty." Of her feelings of inadequacy as a parent, she said, "In a way, it's a kindness and in a way it's showing the kids that mommy can't handle living, and I was feeling very inadequate as a parent." She felt that her husband saw himself as more adequate as a parent and was evaluating her all the time as a parent. G describes her feelings of inadequacy as interfering with her relationship with her children—"I think the parenting thing I was talking about then was so major that I don't think I felt very loving towards them."

A few years after her second son was born, G decided to return to graduate school. She says of this time, "I thought I was happily married," however, during her graduate school program, she became involved with another woman. G is not sure if she was unhappy and didn't realize it or if she began to rethink some of her values and then became unhappy. After becoming involved with another person, she describes herself as "desperate." "My whole life was hanging by a thread." She said of this time, "I don't know if I was that unhappy or just coming to realize it ... what came first?"

G left her husband at that time saying, "I was afraid of him. It was a mental thing, and I don't know why he agreed to let me go if I would agree to come back half a week every week. So I said yes, but as soon as I got out the door, I knew I wasn't going to go back in there. I just did it to get out in the first place."

At the time of the separation, G described herself saying, "I felt stiff, like I didn't feel anything. I was numb. It wasn't me. Rigid, and I wasn't really experiencing this; I was watching." She had some difficulty in the beginning making plans for herself. She said, "So, my thinking processes weren't very clear. I was fragmented, physically and emotionally, as well as in my head." During this difficult period of the separation, G mentioned her husband as a primary support person, "We used to talk on the phone every day."

In addition to her husband, she got support from various friends of whom she said, "One friend let me stay at her house and said her house was my house as long as I needed it and left me alone when I wanted to be alone and was there with me when I wanted to talk." Of another friend, she said, "I knew that no matter what I had done and for what reason this was the one person I could count on." G also briefly mentioned her parents and people at work as being supportive during the time of the divorce.

During the initial stage of the separation, G was still in close contact with her husband. She expressed a conflict between her wanting to go back to her husband and staying with her lover. She said, "I kept being torn between wanting to stay with my husband and, because I felt in love with (friend), wanting to be with (friend). It was a constant being torn from the year before, but that was part of my indecision and not knowing what and always trying to decide what is the right answer and not having a right answer."

In addition to the conflict in deciding between her husband and her lover, she had financial concerns in conjunction with concerns about her children. She said, "The reason I went and he didn't was that I knew on $400 a month I couldn't support the kids and myself, and I knew he made a good salary and we both wanted the kids to have something stable which was the house and at least one parent."

In reference to financial concerns, she was concerned about supporting herself, "I had a job that paid $400 a month, but I was very scared that I couldn't make it on my own." G was also concerned about the financial control her husband had over her. She stated, "The cars were both in his name, and he took my car away from me. I got him to go with me to get a car loan, but I got scared because if he took the car away from me, he could take anything."

G was afraid that her children might be taken away from her because of her affair with another woman. She said of this time, "I was afraid I was going to lose them. I thought they would be told that I was an unfit mother, and I would lose them." In order to give her children some stability during the separation, she said, "I left the house exactly as it was because I wanted the kids to have it like it was. I didn't want their lives to be turned upside down anymore than they had to."

During the separation, G was experiencing enjoyment through her relationship with her lover. She said of that relationship, "I thought my friend was attractive, and I was obsessed with this new relationship. It was unlike anything I had ever known."

After G moved out of her house, she lived with her friend. She said of this time, "I was afraid of being alone. So I leaned on my husband and then I leaned on my friend, and I did that for a long time. Finally, when I was alone, I'd get hysterical. I'd lay on the floor and kick and scream and cry out of absolute terror." Eventually, G sought counseling for herself and came to realize that her emotional turmoil was due to dependency on her part at which point on his advice, "I moved into my own apartment. The therapist is the one who convinced me that I really needed to be living in an apartment by myself and to not immediately want the person that I was seeing to be living with me because he felt that I would understand myself better and know what I really wanted."

G began to feel more comfortable being by herself and said later she began to enjoy the quietness. She said, "Once getting the hysteria over with and seeing that I had survived told me that even in going through that pain that I better start counting on myself," and, "Loved the experience of having peace and quiet and not having to worry at all if it was all right with someone else and doing what I wanted to do." Of being alone now, G says, "As lonely as it can be, I don't think it's the same kind of agony of not being able to make it on my own."

Financially, G became more secure with a professional job which gave her personal satisfaction as well. "Once I started finishing my degree and once I got the job I have now and I was really doing something that I had planned on, I found that I had a part of my life that was intact and functional. I got a lot of reinforcement for what I was doing, and it started to get inside me, so that I could see that it was internal as well as external. I think it's gone from my job to my personal life. This was the first time I had been valued for myself and so I began to value myself for myself."

G and her husband negotiated a co-custody agreement after she moved into her own apartment, but before the boys lived with her, she felt guilty and said, "I'd run to see them in the morning before they were off to school. Then I'd run to my job. I'd be constantly running to assuage my guilt." G has developed positive feelings about her ability to parent in this co-custody arrangement. She said, "It turns out (ex-husband) and I have almost the same kind of parenting ways and attitudes and values. It's very easy for us to support one another." G now feels confident about her parenting and said, "My best experience of parenting was when I was completely on my own."

Socially, G questioned her relationship with her partner and expressed fear about what the future will hold. She said, "I haven't been getting along with my friend. So I may be by myself, and I'm not sure I'll have a partner." G spoke with ambivalence about how she would approach the future socially with, "I think of myself as aging very quickly because of the stress. Then sometimes I think there are plenty of people out there and that I should be more assertive."

G has ambivalent feelings about her ex-husband and their relationship. On the one hand, she recalls the caring, warm, supportive nature of their relationship with, "He's done some things like cut off money because he doesn't think I'm doing something the way he likes or didn't want my friend spending so much time with me." On the other hand, she said, "I don't think I'd go back with him, and then again, there's a part of me that says, boy, if you care for someone still and it goes both ways, who knows." (Subject cries.) G would like to remain friends with her ex-husband, but feels the relationship is constantly changing. She said, "The friendship is still there, but we don't talk everyday the way we used to," and "Our whole relationship is so bizarre."

G felt better about herself at the time of the interview. She said, "I feel stronger about myself." She attributed her good feelings to her professional success. "I'm getting a lot of reinforcement for that and probably the best part of my life is my work right now."

Subject 2B—J

J is 33 years old. She and her husband met while working for the same company. During a ten-year marriage, two sons were born who were seven and nine at the time of the interview. J is now involved in a joint custody arrangement with her ex-husband.

J explained that both she and her husband had come from very similar family backgrounds. Both were described as, "It's the traditional New England family situation. It was bland; there were very few highs and very few lows." She discussed the closeness with her family as, "We've always been very close and still are. We try to get together on every possible occasion." Of her relationship with her in-laws, she said, "Excellent. Rather boring actually."

J said of her marriage, "I can't think of anything I would describe as a problem. I had a very happy mariage, or at least it had all the trappings of a happy marriage." Although J felt her marriage was good, she had some question even before the marriage about her ability to be an adequate marriage partner. She said, "I always loved him, but was never in love with him, and that's what was basically wrong, but I thought there was something wrong with me. I knew I was a misfit in the marriage. I reflected on that at times, but never to the point where I said I was going to leave this marriage."

About five years into the marriage, J became active in the women's movement. She spent most of her non-working hours participating in feminist activities and said of this time, "Frankly, in retrospect, I wanted to escape from my home situation more than I wanted to acknowledge. I felt trapped by the situation (living in the suburbs)."

During J's feminist activism, she said of herself, "I was a big ball of frustration that would sort of go off to these different feminist events leaving (husband) and the kids at home, and I felt guilt about that." J explained that her husband became the primary care giver and was very supportive of her activities.

J discussed her role as parent which was to make all the plans for her children in terms of school and doctors' appointments, while her husband would implement the plan. She said of her children during this period of her life, "During the last few years with (husband), I wasn't really that good of a mother, and I sort of resented the kids."

J recalled feeling guilt about her activist activities and the time taken away from her family and felt she was taking advantage of her husband. J met a woman at a feminist meeting with whom she quickly started an intimate relationship. She said of this relationship, "I realized at the time that I had never been in love with (husband), but once I fell in love with somebody, I realized that I had squelched myself all that time." J decided to leave her marriage shortly after the relationship started. She said, "The minute that I met somebody, it was very clear that I had to make a choice and get out."

During the month between J's meeting her lover and telling her husband she wanted to leave, she faced a great many difficulties. On the one hand she said, "I was so smitten with my new relationship I wasn't thinking very much," and "I was trying to find out if the relationship was going to be permanent." On the other hand, she was feeling guilty and not wanting to hurt her husband. She said, "Getting out with hurting as little as possible, but yet making the break as soon as possible, and I made it."

J also discussed feelings about an amorphous fear of a punishment she was sure she would receive. That fear was connected to her guilt over breaking up the family configuration to live with her lover. She stated, "I just saw myself heading for a great big crash. I don't know if people go through that, but it's knowing that you're going to be punished one day." In response to this fear, J sought counseling as a support for herself during the transition period prior to the divorce.

J recalled isolating herself from other people in terms of telling them about her new relationship and her plans. She did not tell her family or friends about the change until it had been completed. She said, "I suppose isolate is right in that I was playing games with everybody 'cause I didn't let most of my friends know what I was doing."

She described that period of isolation with, "It was like living in two different worlds. In one I had (husband) talk and in the other I had (friend) talk. It was rather bizarre." Although J talked about the difficulties of this period, she did not express any negative feelings about her behavior. She said, "I was so enamored. I was pretty much the blithe spirit. I was so convinced that I was on the right track and happy and nothing could go wrong with my world that my only concern was that (husband) not get tromped on in the process."

A large portion of J's time was spent trying to make sure her husband would not be hurt too much. She said, "I was trying to think of some counseling set-up that (husband) and I could go to together or just him separately so that his transition and anger and what he had to go through could be buffered. Let people know who I thought would have to know, people that I knew who would be able to offer him support the minute I told him. So I spent a month organizing as best I could."

At the time of the final separation, J had no financial concerns other than the complicity of splitting their assets. She and her husband sought advice from a financial advisor and were able to settle this issue amicably. She said, "The financial advisor suggested a few things, but I think the fact that it worked was part luck and part of who we are and how we worked together."

One of her primary concerns was the loss of her children. She felt in a custody suit that she would lose. The result was a joint custody arrangement of which J said, "This situation was actually better than anything I had known." J did experience some difficulty with bringing together her children with her lover and herself. She said, "My friend picked up some of the slack. I actually relinquished some of my responsibility. That developed into some trouble." The difficulty arose over the friend being expected to share responsibility, but being left out of the decision making. Of her relationship with her children now, J said, "I think their perception of me and their enjoyment of me is better too."

At the time of the interview, J expressed satisfaction with her life. She said, "It's so much better than my old life that I think I have succeeded." J also expressed, however, that she has had some difficulty adjusting, but is accomplishing that adjustment in a positive way. She stated, "I think that year of having everything yanked out from under me, all the things that used to be important have been pulled away and changing and living with somebody." J discussed having to rethink her values and change her perception of herself in relationship to her new situation. She said, "I don't feel very valued and then I had to go through a whole process of valuing myself, and that should be good enough, and I'm at the point now where I am what I wanted to be, and I don't have to rely on other people for praise."

J has a special regret about her husband's inability to accept that she did not leave him for another person, but rather because she did not feel comfortable in the marriage. She said, "For (husband's) sake, I wish he didn't connect my leaving him with my having met (friend). I wanted a clean break and then a clean start. I can't do that now. I can't convince him. That's sad."

Subject 3B—T

T is 33 years old. She met her husband during college and married soon after graduation. She and her husband were married for ten years, during which time a son was born who, at the time of the interview, was seven years old. T has been divorced for two years.

T described herself as coming from a traditional Irish Catholic family where the female role was a supportive one. She said, "It was close, but it was rigid Irish Catholic, and you did what you were told. You didn't question, and right and wrong were right and wrong." T attributed the length of her difficult marriage to guilt feelings involved with her feelings about divorce being a step not taken in the Catholic faith. Because of the guilt, T did not communicate with her family concerning her negative feelings about the marriage. She stated, "That had something to say about why there was a cut-off. There was guilt involved with the way I was feeling, and I just sort of stayed away from them."

T met and married her husband while they were attending college. Her family objected to her marriage, but she got their approval after she announced their engagement. She said, "They didn't like him. I just simply stopped talking to them about him, and I simply said at one point that we were getting married."

T described her husband as a star. He was a Rhodes Scholar and was known in his field; however, she also said of him, "He had such an inadequate personality. I thought I could be of some help to him." T also felt that in return for her being supportive of him, she would be secure. She said, "He was a very capable person, and I was totally secure that I would be taken care of."

T transferred her acceptance of the traditional marriage model provided by her parents to her marriage. She stated, "Now that got transferred into my marriage relationship with things like supporting him through school and making no waves about the nature of the relationship." She explained that the nature of the relationship was one of dominance on his part and submissiveness on hers. T felt that her marriage was not an equal partnership and that she was treated as an attractive piece of property. She stated, "I knew that I was supposed to go into traditional family life, but that I didn't really have an existence that was really my own."

T began to raise questions early in the marriage concerning her doubts about the marriage. Her doubts were primarily focused on his treatment of her in terms of public humiliation and putting her down during discussions. She said of that time, "I tried to raise those questions early in the marriage, and he told me that I was crazy and that he loved me and that I was really crazy for thinking that there was anything wrong with the relationship."

T became pregnant and she said of her child, "He didn't want the child, and that it was a major concession on his part to allow me to be pregnant." After the baby was born, T recalled not having any help with the child care and that they moved to Pittsburgh within one year of the delivery.

At about the time of the move, T began to have symptoms of depression. She was tired much of the time and could not sleep or eat. The depression is attributed to her feelings of being trapped by her guilt about not being satisfied with the marriage. She stated, "You're committed for life and the other part of it is that I felt stupid for having made such a mistake."

T started to talk about her situation to her sister and a few friends here in Pittsburgh. She said of her sister, "She called me constantly to see how I was doing or I would call her and one other friend here in Pittsburgh."

In addition to her difficulty with the marriage, T had gotten a job as an instructor at a local university. She was beginning at that time to set some career goals for herself, but was frustrated in attaining them through the lack of support from her husband. She said, "He wouldn't let me stop working to go to school full time. He wanted my pay check. I felt used. He continually used me."

T expressed a general sense of desperation in her relationship with her husband toward the end of the marriage when he took a one year contract in Texas and left her here. She said, "I wanted to be wanted and I wanted him to want to be here. I don't think he wanted me or the marriage, and he certainly didn't want a competent woman who had an opinion or one that would disagree with him." T also wanted to keep the marriage intact even though she had become aware that he was having an affair with another woman in Pittsburgh. She said, "It was humiliating. I felt like a circus animal. If I just did the right thing that he would stay or want to be here."

T's husband requested that she come to Texas to try and hold the marriage together. At that point, T decided that she would stay in Pittsburgh and continue with school.

T explained that she had begun to be able to have some faith in her own judgments through reinforcement at school. This beginning trust in herself gave her the strength to eventually throw off her guilt feelings and file for divorce.

T's relationship with her son during the last two years of the marriage when he was between the ages of 2 and 5 were affected by the depression she was experiencing over the marriage. She said, "I spent time with him mostly around the house in terms of child care or play, but I think at that time I was depressed myself and had little energy." She also said, "We were close and there was a fair amount of concern for him because he was the target of rejection by his father."

T's husband had a difficult relationship with his own family. She recalled times he refused to speak to them on the phone. She said of her relationship with his family, "It was pretty warm and open and caring. I did all the calling and made all the contact."

After a separation, T eventually filed for divorce at the request of her husband. T's reluctance to divorce her husband was explained with, "I wanted out of the marriage, but I didn't want to go to nothing." She also still maintained some thought of reconciliation with: "He was having an affair. Still thinking if I did the right thing he would want to be here."

T recalled after the divorce, "I wanted marriage and I wanted a family life. I didn't have it and I was depressed with the realization that I didn't have it. So I was depressed that I didn't have it." She was fatigued and expressed embarrassment. She said, "The overwhelming amount of energy it took to manage. It was pretty constant. It was a matter of survival from day to day," and "Shame, stigma, embarrassment at work and socially." T summed up this period of her life with, "It was a struggle."

At the time of the divorce, T was concerned about her child and herself as a single parent. She said of her child, "I know that at his age, at that time, I knew enough about child development to know that it is a difficult time—the Oedipal complex." She was not concerned about her ability to parent, but rather the energy it took to work, go to school and take care of her child. She said, "So I had to drop my kid at a baby sitters to get him to school and arrange for someone to get him from the baby sitter to school and from school to the baby sitter after school, pick him up, go home and get dinner and collapse, except I couldn't collapse because I still had to do paper work for my job."

T credits her ability to manage her life in combination with her son to a survival instinct and organizational qualities. She said, "I guess I would say survival instincts and a determination to come through it and figure out difficulties—to make thorough evaluation of the situation before I took any action."

T explained that her son required a lot of attention after the divorce but began to give him more responsibility for himself as time went on. She said, "Gradually I started to give him more responsibility instead of mothering him so much." She says of her time with her son now, "We didn't do too much together and still don't because we cannot financially afford it."

T did not have financial concerns other than her feeling that she could not manage money. She said, "I think I knew I had enough to live on, but I didn't know where it was being spent or how much was allocated to any one place." She solved her management problem with, "I sat down and kept an itemized, and I mean extremely detailed, budget for the lawyer of what I spent and for what for 18 months...So I became very detailed about a lot of things financially."

In terms of her social life, T said, "I didn't give up my social life." T saw herself as attractive and able to function as a dating single person, however, at first, she felt awkward. T was able to begin to feel more comfortable with men, and her new-found confidence in herself through an experience in graduate school. She said, "During the time I was working on my degree, I had chosen to work with men outside the school of nursing. They treated me with respect and treated me as though I had something to offer—that was a break." T has established a stable relationship with another man but has a conflict between maintaining any relationship and, at the same time, being successful in her career. She said, "I still want to get married and have children. Sometimes I think I should give up that notion and grieve the loss and go on and really enjoy my career."

T discussed the decrease in emotional turmoil in the post-divorce period in conjunction with the increase in her self-confidence. She said, "Then it was a question of can I survive, and it took energy keeping it together. Now it's a sense of mastery. More excitement than anxiety." She said her most important lift out of the turmoil came with two realizations. "Finding out I could manage on my own," and "Marriage is a choice."

T explained that although she has grown through the experience of divorce, she is still growing. She said, "I'm a competent person, but I don't know the extent of that, and I have to find out who I am in terms of that. I need to know what my limits are."

At the time of the interview, T was experiencing difficulties in her relationship with her ex-husband. She said, "It's difficult to take a position with him. My ambivalence leads to problems. I still need to be more assertive with him."

Subject 4B—S

S is 29 years old. She graduated from college and enrolled in graduate school. After receiving her Master's degree, she returned to marry a man that she had known since high school and had dated in college. She and her husband were married for 4 years during which time a son was born. At the time of the divorce, her son was 3 years old. S has custody of her son and is now enrolled in a Ph.D. program.

The early part of S's marriage was marked by a series of stressful events. Upon returning from graduate school just prior to her marriage, her mother was diagnosed as having terminal cancer. Her mother was unable to attend the wedding and shortly after the wedding, S, who was a nurse, cared for her mother following an operation during the first week of her marriage. Her husband was unemployed at the time.

S said of that first week, "I remember going into work the first day and seeing people that I knew and one of them asked how married life was, and I said it would be a lot better if we had two bathrooms. So there were feelings even then of something being wrong. That was only after the first week." S attributed her husband's displays of bad temper to the stress of S having to give much of her attention to her mother and her husband's not having a job. She said, "It was during the week that I really saw his temper start to flare. When he got mad at some inconsequential thing, I thought it was due to the temper."

During this early period of her marriage, S also became aware that her husband's family was interfering in their marriage in a controlling fashion. S described one incident, "Little things like going out and buying curtains without asking me that I didn't want and insisting that I put them up even though I didn't like them."

During the first year of their marriage, S recalled her husband becoming "colder, less affectionate, very egotistical and self-centered." In spite of the tension in the marriage, S stated that she and her husband were very social. She said, "When we were out with other people, we had a good time. When we were by ourselves, we didn't."

S began to see that her husband's temper tantrums were becoming worse. "He had temper tantrums so bad he would throw things—frying pans—he would never hit me." She excused his behavior with, "I blamed that on my being the only person working that first year."

Sexually, S described the coldness of her husband by saying, "He was unavailable to me emotionally. Even lovemaking was at his beck and call and clearly when and how he wanted it."

S began to talk to her husband about the difficulties she saw in the marriage. Her husband blamed her. She said, "He would say that everything was my fault and what did I expect from him." S eventually suggested that they seek the services of a marriage counselor and her husband refused. When she threatened to separate if he did not cooperate, she said, "He would threaten me with 'I will commit suicide.'"

S had decided to leave her husband when she discovered that she was pregnant. S said of this time, "Once I got pregnant I said 'Forget this, I can't leave now.'" During the pregnancy and shortly after, her husband's behavior continued to become more bizarre. She said, "He was in military training during the last half of the pregnancy. There were a number of times he could have come home on leave and he didn't." She stated that this behavior was the beginning of her realization that the fears she had early in the marriage that it wouldn't last were becoming a reality.

Two weeks after the pregnancy, her husband was discharged and came home. She said of this time, "No job, a wife and a baby. He went crazy with the responsibility." Because her husband did not have a job, S went back to work three weeks after the baby was born. S described her husband at this time as incapable of making a decision. She said it also bcame clear to her at this time that her husband was probably an alcoholic.

S separated from her husband about four months after her son was born. She described the event which led up to this separation with, "When we got back, he came into the house and found a bottle in the den, at which point he just freaked out. He threw the bottle and the baby carriage off that back porch. Then he threw some other stuff. I didn't know what to say or do." S and her son left the next day. They went to live with a friend.

S lived with her friend for six weeks while she was in the process of convincing her husband to go to a marriage counselor and making an appointment. Eventually, she was able to arrange for her and her husband to go to marriage counseling. During this six-week period, S did not tell her family or other friends that she was separated.

The marriage counselor insisted that S and her husband live together during the treatment. S felt at the time, "It was a big mistake." S described the therapy as being good in that, "I found out in the therapy that other men were in fact warm and loving and tender." A year after the therapy started, S left her husband for the final time. She was separated from him for two years before the divorce was final.

During those two years, S was able to build strength through the support of her family and friends. She said of her family, "Just prior to all of this, my mother had died and my father was alone so he had more time to be supportive, and he was more supportive." S also got support from her older sister. S recalled spending a lot of time with a close friend of hers whom she eventually moved in with for financial reasons. She said of this friend, "I spent time talking to her and other friends. I wondered what people did who didn't have those kinds of people around them. They helped me keep my head on straight and also gave me support in my choice to end the marriage."

S described feeling guilty at the time of the final separation for breaking up the family configuration for her son, but knowing that the situation was not a healthy one for him to be in. She described her financial fears with, "There was a real fear that I wouldn't be able to manage. A real fear that I had was that because of that I would end up going back to him."

S had gone back to work just prior to the final separation and credits this experience with developing positive attitudes toward her self and the situation. She said, "I had a lot of support from the staff people at work." S was able to see, during those two years, that she would be able to manage financially and that she would be able to care for her son.

S described herself as withdrawing socially after the divorce. She said, "I didn't like the bar scene. I didn't cope well. I think I withdrew for about a year."

After the divorce, S enrolled in a graduate program and, at the time of the interview, was pursuing a Ph.D. She said of this decision, "I came back to Pittsburgh because I had some friends here, and I knew I could get some support from them." S is planning to finish her program and move to another area. She said of herself now, "I would like to get out and meet some new people, and I feel more sure of myself now."

Subject 5B—R

R is 32 years old, has been divorced one and a half years. She got married, after graduating from college, to a man who had just completed military service. R has custody of her two children, ages 5 and 6, and is a full-time instructor at a local college.

R's perception of her marriage and relationship to her family, her husband's family and her husband reflects some apparent differences in background. R came from a close-knit, supportive family. She stays in close contact with them and found them supportive during her divorce. She said of her family, "We are a close family," and "We are spread all over the country, but we touch base about once a month, my sister and I. My parents I call about once a week." Her famiy provided support for her during her divorce as they, "checked on me and gave me a few words of comfort. They listened to me when I needed someone to talk to."

In contrast, she felt her in-laws were an unhealthy family configuration and felt as though they did not accept her. She stated, "They were just a little sick, and they disgusted me," and "I tolerated them, and they tolerated me."

R's educational background was also different from her husband's. She was a college graduate while her husband was a high school graduate. It is not clear from the interview, however, that these differences were causes of difficulty in the marriage.

R indicated that difficulties existed early in the marriage when she said, "I knew I had made a mistake two weeks, or, more accurately, two days after the marriage." The difficulties she described centered around her amorphous dissatisfaction with the relationship between herself and her husband and apparent dissatisfaction with herself.

R explained that during the course of the marriage, she felt she could not trust her husband and that she perceived him as not making a commitment to her or the marriage. She said, "Now that I look back on it, he was always looking out for himself. There wasn't much in the way of a real commitment to me or the marriage." R also described feeling as if her marriage had no real substance. She said of her marriage, "Everything we did as a couple or a family was sort of a play," and "We constructed what I thought was a nice middle class existence."

R explained that this middle class existence was based on having done all the right things and acquiring material things. Part of that construction was the births of two sons. R described her relationship with her sons as being happy and bringing her a great deal of joy. She said of her children, "Watching them grow was a wonderful time for me." R expressed regret over having lost the situation that had given her that happiness with, "Sometimes I wish we could go back to the way we used to be, but without him."

R became increasingly unhappy with her marriage over the years and said, "Over the course of the marriage, I became more and more unhappy." In conjunction with the unhappy marriage, R became increasingly unhappy with herself. She describes painful realizations that neither she nor her life would be as she had fantasized they would be. She said of herself, "I would drive to work and my brain would be screaming inside my head saying, 'What's wrong with me.' The feelings of inadequacy were so thick, I could cut them with a knife." Because of her feelings of inadequacy, R felt that she was unattractive to men and that her marriage had been the result of luck. R felt that she would never be happy regardless of her marital state.

R eventually suggested to her husband that they seek marriage counseling. Her husband refused. They began to have several sexual difficulties and did not have sexual relationships at all for the last two years of the marriage. R said of that time, "I even started keeping track of how many times we had intercourse. I stopped keeping track of the times I was rejected."

R began to suspect that her husband was gay. She then began to make the decision to get a divorce. While making this decision, she contacted a lawyer about how to handle the legalities and went to a counselor by herself and told the counselor about her suspicions. She had hoped to get her husband to agree to counseling at that point so that the counselor would tell her husband that she wanted a divorce. R's husband agreed to counseling and, during one of the sessions, he admitted to being bisexual. She said of this time, "I guess I had decided to get the divorce even before I went to the counselor and even more than that I wanted him to tell (husband) that I wanted a divorce."

R described her reaction to her husband's admission of bisexuality with, "Anger, hate, disgust, and joy." R and her husband were divorced shortly after that.

Even though R initiated the divorce, she felt that, "It was the end of the world." She described being extremely lonely and feared that she would always be alone with, "I remember asking the therapist to help me accept the fact that I was always going to be alone and learn to live with it." R had thought about committing suicide as a solution to her loneliness, but felt that she had a responsibility to her children. She said, "I promised myself that after the kids were through college and a little settled that I would cash it in. I refused to spend the rest of my life, until I died naturally, a lonely person."

In reference to being a single parent, R worried about how she would be able to raise them herself. Her most intense reaction to single parenting, however, was resentment. She said, "I resented them for keeping me alive," and "I resented the attention that they needed at a time when I needed to be giving attention to myself." R also explained that she enjoyed some of the time she spent with them and realized that they were keeping her alive and functioning.

R had some brief financial concerns. She was employed at the time, but was not sure she would be able to manage. She stated, "I had a good job, but I knew it was not going to be enough."

R felt that she was physically unattractive and would probably not have a relationship with any other men. She described being extremely lonely and unsuccessful when she did go out. R stated, "I didn't go out a lot and, when I did, I guess I looked too hungry. Men just got turned off. I knew I would never have another relationship again. I was going to be alone for the rest of my life."

During the post-divorce adjustment process, R again expressed the most intense involvement with the emotional aspect of her development. She described functioning in a desperate attempt to keep busy, "Really, I ran around crazy that first year." She discussed how she started to come to terms with her divorce by developing support systems and relying on them to help her adjust. She said, "I also talked to people—friends of mine who were helpful to me by, first of all, being my friend and, secondly, giving me some hints on how to handle things." She also describes not having totally adjusted emotionally, but anticipated finding full satisfaction in her life. She said, "Maybe there isn't, anywhere. Then again, maybe I'm not looking in the right places," and "Someday I'll survive and I'll love it."

In dealing with the financial aspects of her single life, R initially took some practical steps, "By the time the divorce was final, I had rented an apartment and arranged for the kids by having a student live with me while I was working." She describes her lifestyle in a fashion that reflects her ability to live within her means, but alludes to a reduced standard of living with, "I didn't buy any furniture or anything. I lived on hand-me-downs and still do." In the same token, R reflects progress and satisfaction with her financial situation with. "I bought a house with the money, or at least I made a down payment on a house with the rest of the money," and "We manage."

In reference to single parenting concerns, R indicated that she still feels resentment towards her children and still fears that responsibility of their care. She said, "They get in the way sometimes," and "I never know whether or not they are getting all the attention that they need." She is concerned about the welfare of her children and her responsibility for that. She stated, "I love them very much," and "Sometimes I worry about whether or not I'm doing a good job." R indicates that this central theme is still being resolved with, "I've got to stop talking about this. I'm starting to get upset."

R's relationship with her husband, at the time of the interview, was antagonistic, and she felt that he tries to punish her. She said, "I wish he would die," and "He still tries to control me by fooling around with the money."

R discussed her self-esteem at the time of the interview and described a continual growth process which is not complete. She said, "I feel like I've come a long way, but... maybe I'll never get to the end." She indicates a degree of continued unhappiness with, "I want to be happy doing the things I have to do to survive. I'm not happy doing these things."

Subject 6B—E

E is 27 years old. She was married for eight years, during which time a son was born. At the time of the interview, her son, of whom she had custody, was three and one-half years old. E has been divorced two years.

E came from what she describes as being a typical middle class background. She said of her relationship with her parents, "I was a much loved child. I am sure of that." She described her parents' marriage with, "My parents had a good, good marriage. They spoke to me in one voice."

E married a man she had dated in high school and college. Her husband then went into medical school. E says of her marriage, "I had done a praiseworthy thing marrying well." E explained that she thought she was happy being supportive and saw her husband's career as the primary goal. She said, "I adored him and I was very happy to be giving to him. I loved him," and "The real focus was on his career."

During the marriage, E returned to graduate school for a Master's degree. She became pregnant during the program and said, "Up to that point I was very happy visualizing myself as a supporting actress in his life and career." E began to become aware of unmet needs in her life during her pregnancy which were triggered by a rejection of her as a pregnant woman by her husband. She said, "There was no support of me as an imperfect being. He was rejecting of me when I was pregnant. I was offended because I was happy to be pregnant."

E felt at this time that she was not being valued for herself. She said, "I wanted to be adored. I think I wanted to be more of a central character in my husband's life."

After her son was born, E said of herself, "I became very unhappy after (son) was born, and it was a nebulous kind of thing, but desperately unhappy. So desperately unhappy that when I picture (son's) first months, I always get a picture of sitting there nursing him and crying at the same time and tears dropping down onto the baby."

E attributes part of her growing unhappiness to her self-image at the time of the marriage. She said, "My vision was that I was happy because I had somebody to love, and it took me years to question whether somebody loved me," and "What I did was praiseworthy, but by only seeing myself as having gone as far as I could by marrying well, I devalued myself in the classic feminine way."

During the period just prior to the divorce, E spent time talking to a close friend of hers about her feelings. E also was engaged in informal counseling with an instructor she had in her Master's program. She came to realize the depth of her unhappiness through these informal counseling sessions. She said of this time, "I was very troubled and very depressed. It was sort of a post partum depression that I think was post-marital depression delayed."

E thought of herself as being brighter than average and capable of evaluating situations correctly. She evaluated her marriage and said, "My ability to detect bullshit because the way I was living in the marriage was a sham and I was able to see that."

E's relationship with her husband's family during the marriage was described with, "My relationship with his family was good on the surface." She said they liked her very much. E mentioned that, "His mother, who was an important person in that family, liked me." She qualified her statements with, "Maybe she distrusted me a little. She would have preferred someone a little more malleable for her doctor son." However, despite her suspicions of mistrust, E stated that her husband's family took her side in the divorce. She said, "How could he leave this woman and after all he had to be the one who was leaving because how could I leave someone who was such a prize."

The end of E's marriage came very quickly when she discovered that he had been dating other women. She recalls at the moment of discovery that she threw up. She states, "My whole body rejected the idea." She explained that although the dissolution of the marriage was the result of the affair, neither she nor her husband could say that they had been happy for a long time.

E described the period between her discovery of her husband's affair and their final separation a few months later with, "We decided to separate on a

Sunday night. The anxiety, the tension and the pain were incredible. It's physical, it's emotional, it's total. Inability to sleep. Almost the inability to move. "I felt like my life was over. I wanted to die." She explained that she felt pain, but not bitterness or anger toward her husband with, "Neither of us wanted to sleep with the other one anymore, and I simply couldn't blame him for wanting someone who loved him more than I did."

E's primary concern at the time of the final separation was her fear of being alone. She explained, "Not a physical fear of burglars but an emotional fear of being alone and not having someone to talk to and not having someone to bounce my ideas off of." She also stated the need for a sexually intimate relationship with, "I had never not been in an intimate relationship. That was paramount. I'll have to have another sexual relationship in my life." E felt that not having intimacy emotionally and sexually would be painful.

E became involved with another man shortly after the separation. She credits her coming out of the pain of the divorce to this man. She explained that at the time of the divorce she felt ugly, stupid and asexual. E further explained the development of self-confidence was also due to this man. She said, "I wished I could say I forged my personality myself, that I rose like a phoenix from my own ashes, but I didn't."

E felt that, although she had moved away from the pain to some extent, she said, "I see myself as still coming out. I think it takes years to get over a divorce. I think I'm still getting over it."

E said of her financial situation, "The time I worried about finances or support or where my next meal was coming from was very short." She stated, "I made what I considered a very good financial deal," and "Things have only been better since financially."

E experienced ambivalence in terms of her son. She loved him, but at the same time, felt that he was a great responsibility. She said, "During most of the early part of it, because I just didn't look at him ... It was if I super loved him. He had this almost too important place in my life and I couldn't stand his being around. Both things at the same time." She felt positively about her son's part in keeping her alive. She said, "If it hadn't been for him I would have wanted to kill myself." E had no fears about being a single parent. She stated, "All mothers are single parents." E was satisfied and comfortable as a parent at the time of the interview. She stated, "I have absolute confidence in my ability to deal with whatever comes up with him, and I think he's lucky to have me for a mother." She explained that, although she had confidence in her parenting abilities, parenting was not her primary goal. E felt that her life, in general, would be more satisfying if she were in a position to make more money and if she were involved in a permanent, stable relation with a man. She said, "When I have those other two things, everything will fall in place with my son."

E stated that she was experiencing difficulty in establishing a new relationship with her ex-husband. She said, "There's some antagonism that's associated with (son)." She sees the antagonism as a reaction against her. She stated, "A way of controlling my life." E also commented that she has changed in ways that have changed her feelings about her ex-husband with, "He's not the sort of person I like."

General Descriptions

The descriptive statements, descriptive summaries and data charts were examined to develop a general description of three areas of the divorce experience:

1. Pre-divorce conditions;
2. Central themes;
3. Resolution of themes in post-divorce adjustment.

The following is the general description of pre-divorce conditions among working class women:

General Description of the Pre-divorce Conditions Among Working Class Women

The discussion of the pre-divorce experience of the marriage provided information for the initial research questions, but also proved to be invaluable in determining differences between the two groups regarding the total experience of divorce. Also, the construction of the general descriptions gave a general impression of the level of involvement the women had in each area of the pre-divorce conditions, making it possible to see a relationship between the pre-divorce conditions and the experience of divorce and post-divorce adjustment.

Pre-divorce experience of marriage. Among working class women, comments were made that left the general impression that the marriage itself rather than the relationship between husband and wife was of primary importance. G discussed wanting the marriage all her life. She said, "I had grown up wanting that (the marriage), and I made up my mind that I was going to have that home and so I felt I couldn't leave because that was giving up that dream that I wanted so badly, and besides that, I had two little kids." L felt the social expectation for her was to be married and she said, "I liked being married." M felt that she had time invested in her marriage with, "I really didn't want the marriage to end because we had been married this long." Although U had been beaten repeatedly and her husband had informed her of an affair he was having, she said, "I was trying to keep things together, work, take care of (son) and take care of (husband). I wasn't thinking about a divorce." J said simply, "I was more in love with love than with my husband." T saw her marriage as a way of escaping from her family. She said, "Really, I just married him to get away."

The women in this group ascribed to the rigid traditional conjugal roles of marriage. It was accepted by these women that their husbands would be the head of the household, and the decision maker. They understood that they would be responsible for child care and domestic duties. G said, "(Husband) was really important." L stated, "He was from the old school and so was I. He was the lord, the master." M said, "He didn't want to do anything. He believed you go to work and then come home and eat and lay on the couch and watch TV, and he took care of the car." U said, "Everything seemed to go smoothly in the beginning." J said, "He was like you do what I say or else." T stated, "He told me to go to work, and I went to work."

The women in this group expressed being happy in their marriages, with the exception of J and T, as long as their husbands remained within the boundaries of the traditional roles. Incidences occurred within all of the marriages early in the relationships which the women viewed as negative, but not to the extent that they would consider divorce. G, for instance, discovered that her husband lied to her several times and had been sexually abused by her husband for several years during the marriage. L's husband restricted her efforts to develop a career and painfully insulted her in the process. M felt that in decision making her husband did not respect her opinions and, in addition, felt that she shouldered more than her share of the responsibility for the marriage. U's husband socialized without her, contributing to her feelings of neglect.

In spite of negative behaviors, these women said they had good marriages or that they were happy. G said, "I was happy myself, but it really pleased me because I thought everyone else thought my marriage was perfect, and they were getting something out of it." L said, "We were a close knit family." M said, "We had a good marriage," and U stated, "It was good in the beginning."

J and T were not happy in their marriages, but felt that they should remain in the marriage to avoid the social embarrassment of a divorce. J said, "I knew my mother would say it serves you right," and T said, "My mother would say, you made your bed now lie in it."

The women in this group became unhappy with their marriages only after they had discovered that their husbands had stepped outside the boundaries of expected behavior by becoming sexually involved with another woman. J and T were the exception, but both of them felt their husbands had also stepped outside the boundaries—J's husband by insisting she get an abortion and T's husband by sexually and emotionally harassing her.

Inner strengths. During the interview when the women were asked what they felt were strengths that helped them through the difficulties of the divorce, all of the women made comments such as, "I never thought about that," or "I don't know." Following these comments, the women addressed themselves to what they saw as developing into strengths after the divorce.

After pursuing the subject of pre-divorce inner strengths, some of the women made comments which indicated that they felt they were more responsible and mature than their husbands.

G compared herself to her husband by saying, "I had personality. I was more outgoing and got along with people easier." G also found that during a separation prior to the divorce, she began to gain more confidence. She said, "I had more confidence during that year because of this job and finding out that I could do something, but still wanted both (job and marriage)." M compared her level of responsibility to her husband's. She said, "I guess before the divorce, during all that time that I was married, I carried all the responsibility." U stated simply that she was more mature and responsible than her husband with, "I can constantly keep a job and he can't. I pay my bills and he doesn't." T felt she was more intelligent than her husband and came from a higher socio-economic group. She said, "I married a man who was a lot stupider than I was."

L found most of her strength after the divorce. She said that she thought she needed to depend on a man. However, during the marriage, "I started changing and becoming more independent, asserting myself and challenging him." Later in the interview, however, L discussed that she was afraid she might become too strong and feared the loss of her femininity.

J credited the impending birth of her daughter as giving her strength. She said, "The thing I saw most is that I wanted (daughter) really, you know, a lot. I think the fact that she was coming along made it even better." J also being able to protect herself emotionally said, "I think I put up a shield, and I wasn't about to let it fall. I can protect myself that way."

Support systems. All of the women in this group received support prior to and during the divorce from two sources: (1) from close friends and (2) from their families. The support from friends came in the form of verbal support. Support from family was more active.

The women in this group, with the exception of L, discussed their problems first with friends. Often the family was not informed until the decision was made or they needed financial help. All of the women, including L, felt that they had either disappointed their families or would be ridiculed by them.

G said, "I couldn't talk to my grandmother about it. She had had enough trouble." L said, "I felt like I had let society down." These two women had a sense of failure, although L had contact with her family about the situation immediately after her husband announced that he wanted a divorce.

M did not have a feeling that she had disappointed her family, but feared becoming a burden to them. She asked her mother for money to leave her husband, which was sent immediately. She said of living with her family, "It was hard and then my grandfather moved in with us."

J, U and T feared ridicule from their families. They stated that they would be subjected to an "I told you so attitude." However, the families of each of these women gave them immediate support when finally asked.

All of the women in this group had a special friend or friends they confided in prior to the divorce. L, however, stated, "They came out of the woodwork." She said she got support from people she never suspected would give it to her.

Relationship with husband during the marriage. Each of the women in this group discussed the good parts of their relationship with their husbands, but as the interview continued, they began to discuss behavior in their husbands that they considered to be negative. None of the negative behavior, however, precipitated the divorce.

G started a discussion of her relationship with her husband with, "We got along well. I genuinely liked him." Further into the interview, she began to talk about his sexually abusing her. She said, "That was one way he knew that he could hurt me, so it still upsets me. It makes me angry . . . It was humiliating." G recalled that she found out her husband had been having sexual relations with her sister's friend. She separated from him for a year after that, but reconciled with the idea that she could salvage the marriage. A few months after the reconciliation, she found out that he had propositioned her sister. She still tried to get her husband to go to marriage counseling and when he refused she asked him to leave. She said of that time, "I couldn't live with him anymore."

L discussed her relationship with her husband as one of dependence on him. She described their relationship with, "We were friends." L decided to brush up on her secretarial skills and get a job. She described her relationship as starting to change when she started to go to school. She said, "I was told my dreams were silly. I got rejection from him and rejection from the employers. Instead of encouraging me he would tell me I was up against young girls." L's husband expected her to work and keep up with all her domestic duties as well. She began to gain some confidence in herself through the job, at which point her husband announced that he wanted a divorce to marry another woman. From that point on, their relationship deteriorated to a point two weeks later when they stopped communicating with each other. L said, "He completely turned his back on me. The only communication we have is through lawyers."

M expressed a feeling of satisfaction with the marriage. She said, "I guess it was just nice being together. We could talk." She pointed out that in the talking that "He always had to be right. I didn't know anything and he knew everything." M resented her husband's refusal to become involved in any responsibilities other than work and fixing the car. She stated that later in the marriage he decided he would hold all the money, and it was at that point she discovered his affair. Her husband asked her for a divorce, but she stayed with him until the financial situation became so bad that "I went down to the neighbor's house and she fed the kids. There was no food." She left her husband, but wished that somehow they "could have worked it out."

U also said "It seemed to work out fine (in the beginning)." After U gave birth to her son, her husband told her he was having an affair and started to beat her. She said, 'He tried to strangle me about five times." U left her husband for a short period of time and decided "to go back and try and make a go of it." He had been taking drugs and started to beat her again. She now lives with her ex-husband and her ex-in-laws. She said of this arrangement, "I saw it as a golden opportunity to give back what he gave me." The relationship is now antagonistic.

J's marriage started with a long separation during which her husband was stationed in Turkey. Before he was transferred, she described his treatment of her with, "He was like—oh, anything you want we'll get." After his return, she described his treatment of her with, "He was like the type where what I say goes, and if you don't like it then that's too damn bad." J stated that her husband was a heavy drinker and his behavior was unpredictable during those times. She also recalled being humiliated in public by her husband. After she got pregnant, her husband insisted she get an abortion. It was at that point that she decided to leave.

T described her husband as being available at a time when she needed a vehicle to escape from her family. She described her relationship with him with, "Sexually he made my life a nightmare." She discussed behavior on his part which indicated to her that he wanted complete dominance over her. Early in the marriage, she became unhappy with the relationship, but remained in that marriage for several years.

Relationship with the children. The relationship of the women in this group was related to the role of parenting assumed by women in the traditional marriage pattern among the working class. J was the exception in that her daughter was born during a separation that ended with a divorce.

G, L and M promoted their children's relationship with the father. They viewed their relationship with their children not as a personal relationship, but rather a family relationship. G said, "I was raising them for him." L said, "We did a lot of things together as a couple and with our children." M said, "It was nice, the family things we did together." All three of these women talked about negative aspects of that relationship, and, for G and M, these negative parts of the relationship were directly related to tension in the marriage. G said, "I was very nervous and very irritable, and I didn't abuse them, but I don't think I took the time with them I should have." M said, "When all this trouble built up on me, I beat them. I beat them a lot." L stated that during the marriage she took her children for granted and didn't get as involved with their lives as she is now.

T had a limited relationship with her daughter. She and her husband were heavy into drugs and spent evenings out leaving the child with a baby sitter. During the day, the child was in a day care center. When asked how she felt about her daughter before the divorce, T said, "I couldn't feel anything when I was married to him."

Relationship with in-laws. Two of the women, G and T, had especially hostile relationships with their mothers-in-law. G described her relationship with, "If she didn't get her way, she'd get migraine headaches." T described her relationship with, "His mother hated me." T recalled having physical confrontations with her mother-in-law.

Both M and J were married to men whose mothers had died. Their contact in both cases was with a sister of the husband's. M's in-laws would visit with her and her husband during the marriage. After the marriage, M said, "She just can't accept what he did." J had very little contact with her husband's family, but said of them, "They were just happy that he had found someone to settle down with."

L was unusual in this group in that she had and still has a very close relationship with her in-laws. She said of them after the divorce, "They took my side. His mother still calls me to this day and cries."

Relationship with family of origin. L is unusual in the group in regard to her relationship with her family. She described this relationship as being very close all through her life. She said of them, "I'm not the first to get a divorce, and we get along great." After the divorce, she said of them, "They gave me a lot of support through all of this."

The other women in the group give the impression that they perceive their relationship with their families as being emotionally noncommitted. G was sent to live with her grandmother and although close to her she said, "I was lonely all my life. I felt rejected." G left her mother after her step-father sexually abused her. She saw her mother as, "A whiner and a complainer." M describes herself as being independent and not able to live with her family. She said, "I shared a lot of these problems with them." She did not get support for her efforts to come back to school. "My grades are good, and my dad never thought I could make it. He doesn't really care, and you know, we don't discuss it much." U stated that she didn't want to stay with her family either. She said of them, "Once you leave the nest, you don't go back." She also credited her family with helping her through the difficult months after the divorce. J, who also moved in with her mother, said, "My mother was and is real protective." J resents having to live with her family and resents the restrictions placed on her by her mother. She said of her relationship with her mother, "One simple word—like hell. It was not a good relationship and not even now." T described her mother as "mentally ill," and her father as being "in his own little world." She spoke fondly of them but did not expect to get any support from them. T did not move in with her family after she left her husband and, although on welfare, maintains her own apartment.

This general description points to high levels of involvement in the marriage with the husband and with the children for most of the women in this group. It also points to lower levels of involvement in recognition of inner strength and support systems, as well as with the family of origin. The lack of emotional commitment between the family of origin and the working class women in this study was a source of anger and resentment for some of the women. This relationship, however, was also perceived as promoting the need for the women to make decisions about their lives independent of their families early in the post-divorce adjustment period. The necessity of making independent decisions, in turn, gave the women much needed confidence in their ability to survive.

General Description of Pre-divorce Conditions of Marriage Among Middle Class Women

The development of the general description for middle class women also provided information concerning level of involvement in the marriage and provided valuable information for a clear understanding of the divorce experience. Also, this description further illustrated the uniqueness of each group's experience of the pre-conditions of divorce.

One notable characteristic of the pre-divorce experience of the middle class was the questioning by the women of the quality of the marriage relationship early in the marriage. Another significant finding is that women in the middle class commented on their lack of identity and self-esteem during the marriage. Therefore, a separate category labeled self-esteem was added to the general description of the pre-divorce experience for the middle class women.

Self-esteem during the marriage. Although self-esteem during the marriage was not suggested by the literature as one of the significant pre-divorce conditions affecting post-divorce adjustment, it became evident through an examination of the data that it was a vital part of the middle class women's experience of their marriages. In relating their pre-divorce experience, each of the women consistently referred to how interaction with their husbands made them feel about themselves. For instance, T related that, "I had very little confidence and self-esteem. He could put me down real fast and make me feel stupid." S concurred with, "... before the divorce and during the marriage, my self-esteem was down there on the floor someplace... he would always talk me down."

Some of the women related that they had come into the marriage with feelings of low self-esteem which increased through interaction with their husbands, as in G's case, who said, "I didn't have a lot of adequate feelings to start with, and his sureness about himself and his sureness about how inadequate I was in certain areas would reinforce some of the negative feelings." E related her feelings of inadequacy to a general attitude toward herself as a woman, which was also reinforced by her relationship with her husband. She said, "I had a fairly poor self-image when I married for certain things. I devalued myself in the classic feminine way." E had been taught that her greatest accomplishment as a woman would be to marry well. She did, in perception, marry well, but found that her husband valued her for her appearance and support of him rather than for the "things I valued in myself."

J was the exception in that prior to the divorce she felt confident about her self. She imparted this impression with, "I had always been a leader..."

Pre-divorce experience of the marriage. For three of the women in this group, G, T and E, the nature of their feelings of inadequacy was related to how they perceived their marriages initially. The three women viewed themselves as being inadequate as E pointed out, "in the classic feminine sense," that is to say that they viewed their value as women to be their ability to marry well and to be made secure through that marriage. Each of these women commented that their husbands had been as G put it, "a good catch."

Each of these women also experienced themselves becoming increasingly unhappy during the course of the marriage. They each, in turn, tried to question that unhappiness only to realize the amorphous quality of it. They reasoned that they really had no reason to be unhappy because they had married well. G said, "I didn't feel good about myself, and the marriage wasn't that good either, but I kept pushing it away because he was a good catch." T said, "He was a very capable person, and I was totally secure that I would be taken care of... I knew I was supposed to go into traditional family life, but that I didn't really have an existence that was really my own." E said, "and because of the fact that I had been brought up to think that I had done a very valuable thing to marry a doctor and that it seemed appropriate to postpone gratification for years and years, and it seemed right."

The experience of R was similar with the exception that she felt so inadequate and unattractive that she considered herself lucky to have married at all. She said, "I thought I was lucky to have gotten married in the first place..." R was aware of her unhappiness early in the marriage, but feared being alone for the rest of her life.

The growing sense that they were not being valued as persons in the marriage was a common realization to all of the women. This growing unhappiness was reinforced by incidences of humiliation, experienced by all these women, by their husbands. G said, "I remember times he'd throw food on the floor, and I'd go and clean it up, and I took it." T said, "It was humiliating. I felt like a circus animal. If I just did the right thing that he would stay or want to be there." R said, "I started to keep track of the times we had intercourse. I stopped keeping track of the times I had been rejected." E said, "He was rejecting of me when I was pregnant. I was offended because I was happy to be pregnant."

Although S stated that she had a low self-esteem, she gave the impression that it was a result of the relationship between her husband and herself. She recalled that he had temper tantrums and when she questioned his behavior and the need to discuss these difficulties, she said, "He would always talk me down." S knew from the beginning of the marriage that it was not going to work out. She continued in the marriage by rationalizing his behavior and blaming it on stress that he was under due to being unemployed.

J was unique in that she felt her marriage was excellent. Her growing dissatisfaction developed, not with the marriage, but with boredom. She said, "I felt trapped in the suburbs." She did not feel inadequate or insecure before or during the marriage. In order to relieve the boredom, she became enthusiastically involved in the women's movement. She eventually met and fell in love with another women who was in much the same situation J was in. J's marriage ended shortly after the new relationship started.

All of the women in this group experienced varying degrees of sexual dissatisfaction with the marriage. G recalled that sexual relations in her marriage were, "O.K. It was good sometimes and sometimes it was just all right." J felt that she was not a warm and affectionate partner, but did not mention any particular difficulties. T accepted her husband's lack of sexuality during the marriage based on religious beliefs that promoted sexuality for procreation and not for enjoyment. She said of her husband, "He didn't exude sex. He was asexual." S perceived her husband as cold and insensitive. She said, "Even lovemaking was at his beck and call and how and when he wanted it." R's husband was a homosexual. She recalled that at one point in the marriage the infrequent sexual activity she had experienced stopped completely. She said, "I started keeping track of the times we had intercourse. I stopped keeping track of the times I had been rejected." E simply stated, "If our marriage failed in any way, it failed sexually." Later in the interview each of the women talked about how much better, in comparison, their sexual relationships had become.

Unlike other women in the group, J and E discussed being happy in their marriages for several years. J stated that her marriage was "excellent. There was nothing I would call a problem." E said, "I think for most of the eight year period I was married, at the time, I thought of myself as happy." In retrospect, however, both of these women pointed to areas of dissatisfaction. J said, "I always loved him, but was never in love with him and that was what was basically wrong... I just wasn't aware that love was the missing ingredient." E said, "There was no depth to (husband's) feelings for me, although I think he has good feelings for me."

G described her marriage as being "good at times and parts of it were not so good." At certain times during her marriage, she described being happy. She said of one of those times, "It (going back to school) had a good effect on the marriage. We began to do things together. It was almost like a merging." Of one of the bad times, she said, "When I started to stay home (after birth of her first child), there was more tension between us, and he was like a little boy feeling jealous and wanting more attention."

J, T and R described themselves as being dissatisfied in the marriage almost from the beginning. Both J and R made statements about having doubts within days of the marriage. J said, "So there were feelings even then of something being wrong. That was only after a week." R said, "I knew I had made a mistake two weeks or, more accurately, two days after the marriage." T said, "I tried to raise those questions early in the marriage, and he told me I was crazy and that he loved me and that I was really crazy for thinking that there was anything wrong with the relationship."

Both S and R had similar feelings about maintaining a social facade during the marriage. R said, "When we were with other people we had a good time. When we were by ourselves we didn't." R stated, "Everything we did as a couple or a family was sort of a play."

Inner strengths. When asked what they saw as strengths in themselves that helped them cope with the difficulties of the divorce, five of the women, G, S, J, T and E, responded by pointing to their success or anticipated success professionally. In addition, two of those women, G and T, described themselves as much stronger since the divorce as a direct result of having gotten away from the influence of their husbands.

In reference to professional strength, G said, "I think it was not personal strength that I recognized now, but career strength. I was very good and competent." In retrospect, G stated, "I think I had to get out from under and get out and see what my strengths were." Similarly, T said, "A beginning ability to kind of trust in my own judgment (professionally) which has since become very solid." T pointed to men in her professional area who respect her abilities and gave her positive reinforcement.

J, S and E discussed professional strengths they saw in themselves prior to the divorce which were, at the time of the interview, still recognized as strengths. J said, "I had always been a leader by working in traditional male fields." She also said of herself, "There was no insecurity." S said, "I think that's where I got my self-confidence professionally and once I had gotten that professionally, I could adapt that to my personal life." E stated, "I was highly employable."

The women discussed other strengths which were unique to them individually. G felt that she was flexible. J and T described themselves as being able to organize well. R and E thought of themselves as being intelligent.

Support systems. All of the women in this group initially started building a support system with personal counseling. They all engaged in therapy prior to the divorce before telling friends and family about the anticipated divorce. Of all the women, only S and T engaged in marriage counseling. The personal counseling in all cases started prior to the divorce, continued through the divorce and terminated some time after. The counseling was credited with helping them realize the origins of their unhappiness and to cope with the divorce.

With the exception of J and E, the other women built support systems of friends and family. G included her husband as a support for her also. She said, "He was my support for a long time, and my friend was, and some select people that I knew." The women with whom G started a relationship with prior to the divorce gave her support by staying with her and talking with her, but G described a very special friend with, "She lived very far away, but I called her and told her what I had done and she wrote to me and let me know how much she loved me." T described a supportive relationship with "My sister. She called me constantly to see how I was doing, or I called her and one friend here in Pittsburgh. I had someone to talk to." S credited a close friend and other friends with helping her develop the courage to get the divorce. She said, "They helped me keep my head on straight and also gave me support in my choice to end the marriage." Of her family she said, "They (sister and father) were very supportive." R described supportive friends with, "I had three good friends who gave me a lot of help and were always there for me to talk to." Of her family, she said, "They listened to me."

E and J gave the impression of isolating themselves from family and other than very close friends. Both shared their difficulties with a counselor and a close friend. E said of her friend, "I had one extremely close woman friend, and I doubt my ability to have gotten through this without that relationship." J stated that she had no support and isolated herself, but she and the woman she was involved with shared many of the same difficulties. She said, "Of course, (friend) was going through all of this at the same time." Both J and E did not inform their parents until after they had separated from their husbands just prior to the divorce. Both women described their parents as not understanding what they had been through and not able to give them any support.

Relationship with husband. Three of the women, T S and E, described relationships with their husbands which gave the general impression that they felt unloved in the relationship and further that they were somehow being used by their husbands. All three of these women also financially supported their husbands during part of the marriage. T felt that her husband thought of her as an object. She said, "A physically attractive accoutrement rather than a great deal of shared pleasure around that. I felt used. He continually used me." S said of her husband, "He became colder, insensitive, less affectionate, very egotistical and self-centered. He would say it was all my fault..." Although S perceived her husband as less affectionate towards her, he threatened to commit suicide if she left him. E had a much longer history with her husband, and she said of him, "I adored that boy and I have to say that boy because I started seeing him when I was sixteen." However, later in the marriage, she said of him, "There was no support of me as an imperfect being. It was that I wasn't valued."

T described herself as living a separate existence in the marriage. She felt that he had made no commitment to the marriage or to her. She said of him, "I always had the feeling that I couldn't trust him." Of the relationship itself, she said, "Everything we did as a couple or a family was sort of a play."

G was ambivalent about her relationship with her husband. On the one hand, she described him as a best friend. She said, "I still get weepy about him and the caring that went on between us." On the other hand, she described him as being critical of her, "Every once in a while, he'd get upset over the simplest things, mostly around food. I remember times he'd throw food on the floor and I'd go and clean it up, and I took it." G described herself as being dependent on her husband and feeling sorry for him by being a burden on him. She said, "I never made a decision. He had to make them all. You can imagine what a burden that must have been." G recalled, "I made that up to him by never saying no." The relationship became more complicated when G began to resent what she felt she had to do to please her husband.

J and her husband had an excellent relationship. She described him with, "Very supportive of everything I was doing and tried to take part. He was super understanding." J felt guilty about taking advantage of her husband's "good nature" while participating in her activities outside the home. At the time of the interview, she said of her husband, "he's such a sweet guy. He still cares about me..."

Relationship with children. Among the middle class women in this group, a pattern emerged regarding the relationship with the children and the women's growing dissatisfaction with the marriage. The more unhappy the women were in the marriage, the less satisfactory were their relationships with their children.

G saw herself as inadequate in the marriage but felt that she would be a wonderful parent. She began to realize that caring for children required a great deal of hard work. G also saw her husband as evaluating her ability as a parent and finding her lacking. In his evaluation, she saw him as invading her role of a parent and being better at it than she was. G said of this situation, "Sometimes he'd look at me and watch me with them, and I know he was evaluating me, always evaluating me and my competence in it, and so sometimes he'd press his hand in a downward motion and that was to tell me to cool it because I wasn't handling it right, and he would take over." Because of the feelings of inadequacy as a parent, G's relationship with her children was not close. She said, "I think the parenting thing I was talking about then was so major that I don't think I felt very loving towards them." G felt she fulfilled her role as a parent, but did not derive pleasure from it. She said, "I did things for and with them because I thought it was something I should do, and it was more of a should than a want."

J's relationship with her children was "excellent" until she began to feel trapped in her suburban housewife role. She became active in the feminist movement during the last few years of her marriage. She perceived her children as needing attention, but perceived herself as needing the outside activities for herself. She said, "During the last few years with (husband), I really wasn't that good of a mother and I sort of resented the kids." In terms of her needs, J said, "I was a big ball of frustration that would sort of go off to these different feminist events leaving (husband) and the kids at home, and I felt guilt about that." The guilt J referred to, however, was more about taking advantage of her husband than with leaving the children.

T described her relationship with her child as being close in that she did the care giving while he was young. However, prior to the divorce, T described her decreased ability to do much more than care giving with, "I spent time with him mostly around the house in terms of child care or play, but I think at that time I was depressed myself and had little energy." T perceived herself and her son as being rejected by her husband, but said, "He probably spent more time with his father in the way of going out and having a good time than he spent with me."

E's son was born a few months before the final separation from her husband. She related having gone through his babyhood without her being actively involved with his growth. Of his early months she said she was, "so desperately unhappy that when I picture (son's) first months, I always get the picture of sitting there nursing him and crying at the same time and tears dripping down onto the baby." She said, "It was as if I super loved him and could not stand his being around."

R and S described being close to their children prior to the divorce and enjoying their growth. R said, "Watching them grow was a wonderful time for me." S said, "I spent a great deal of time with him in terms of child care." R voiced regret over the loss of that time for her with, "Sometimes I wish we could go back to the way we used to be, but without him."

Relationship with in-laws. Relationships with the husband's family followed two distinct patterns. One pattern described the relationship as warm and caring. These relationships were in some instances carried beyond the divorce. The second pattern described a negative relationship in which the women felt uncomfortable.

In the positive relationships, the women described situations of mutual caring and reciprocated respect. G had known her husband's family for many years and said that, "Everybody treated me very warmly." T had become involved with caring for her mother-in-law in her capacity as a nurse. J perceived her husband's family as being much like hers in that they were also a traditionally New England family and described the relationship as "excellent." E felt that her relationship was "good on the surface" and that her mother-in-law "liked me very much." However, she felt that her mother-in-law perceived her as being too strong a person for her "doctor son."

In the negative patterns, S saw her in-laws as resenting her for taking their son "out of the nest." S perceived them as interfering and attempting to exert control over the marriage. T described her relationship as mutually intolerable. She described his family as "a little sick and they disgusted me." Both of these women described their husbands in generally the same way.

Relationship with family of origin. All of the women in this group described close relationships with their families. E used the term "much loved child" and J said, "We were always close." However, in some cases, the women perceived negative aspects of those relationships which when transferred to their marriages caused difficulty.

G, for instance, saw her family as demanding and treating her as a "sixteen year old." She perceived her husband as being demanding at times and not feeling she was capable. J said of her family that painful situations are not talked about, a situation she encountered in her attempts to "escape" without hurting her husband. T's family was "rigid Irish Catholic, and you did what you were told." In her attempt to try and live that way in her marriage, she became unhappy. As in T's case, preparation for marriage created problems for E also. E's parents had brought her up to believe that marrying well would be her greatest achievement. She became dissatisfied with that level of accomplishment.

This general description points to high levels of involvement in the pre-divorce conditions, except in the areas of support systems and inner strengths. This particular finding was found also among working class women. However, it also points to a significant difference between the two groups in terms of values and attitudes toward the marriage. It was illustrated that middle class women expected an egalitarian approach to marriage.

The unanticipated emergence of low levels of self-esteem during the marriage as a central theme is indicated in the general descriptions. This theme appears to be related to the egalitarian value system in middle class marriages in conjunction with lack of support from the husbands of these women in their quest to establish an identity.

Further, this description indicates two different mother-child relationships. In some cases, the relationships with the children were negative during the marriage, while others were positive. The negative relationships were seen as a function of the dissatisfaction with the marriage.

In some cases, among the middle class, that expectation was present before the marriage and, in other cases, developed during the marriage. Further, the expectation of equal consideration in the marriage was in many cases a primary contributing factor in the dissolution of the marriage by the women.

General Description of Central Themes Among Working Class Women

In developing the general description of central themes for working class women, it was anticipated that differences would occur, not in regard to the actual central themes, but in terms of how those themes were experienced. However, it became apparent that two themes, not previously anticipated, were surfacing during a review of the descriptive statements.

One theme pertained to feelings of low self-esteem at the time of the divorce. A separate category was then given to this theme for working class women.

The second theme had to do with establishing a new relationship with the ex-husband. Although this theme was actually discussed by the women during the post-divorce adjustment, it was seen as a central theme of divorce and a separate category was given to it also.

Interpersonal concerns—emotional reaction to final separation. During the discussion of their pre-divorce experience of their marriage, three of the women, G, L and M, stated clearly that they had good marriages and were happy in them. U said her marriage was good in the beginning and both J and T were unhappy in their marriages. Further, the general impression given by the interviewees is that G, L, and M were highly involved in their marriages and, although T was unhappy, she also was highly involved. U and J gave the impression of not being highly involved.

Each of the three women who were highly involved in happy marriages, described themselves as feeling frightened, disappointed, sorry for themselves and as if their worlds had been destroyed. G, whose husband had been sexually involved with other women, said, "(I was) disappointed for letting it happen. It was frightening." L concurred with, "I felt like my whole world was crumbling in on me." M added, "I cried all the time." Unlike the other three women, T was unhappy in her marriage. She was, however, highly involved with that marriage and had reactions similar to intensity, but of relief. She said, "I was exalted. I was just so happy to get out of there.'

U explained that after her son was born, her husband announced he was in love with another woman and would beat U on frequent occasions. After the beatings started, she described herself as being anxious and nervous. At the time of the divorce, she reacted with, "I was angry and resented him. I felt I was hurt."

J had been unhappy in her marriage and had a less severe reaction. J became angry for a short time after receiving the divorce papers served by her husband.

Guilt at having caused the difficulties in the marriage was part of the emotional reaction for those women whose husbands initiated the divorce in order to continue a relationship with another woman. L blamed her behavior as the cause by saying, "Maybe I should have handled that differently or maybe I should have said that." M described her inability to remain attractive with, "When there is no money, you can't buy the clothes you want." U simply said, "I blamed myself." Although G's husband had not initiated the divorce, he also had been involved sexually with other women. She did not feel guilt but shared a feeling of rejection with these other women.

Still another reaction shared by several of the women was loneliness. G described herself as being "frightened of being alone." L and U felt lonely, but did not express fear.

A sense of failure was also described by G and L. G feared she had disappointed her family because "They all thought I had a perfect marriage." L was not concerned about her family but felt she "had let society down."

U voiced her anger and resentment toward her husband as her initial reaction. This reaction, although not the initial reaction, was shared by M who "had nightmares of killing him," and G, who said, "I can talk to him now without hating him."

When it became accepted by the women that divorce was inevitable, disbelief was a shared reaction. Comments such as "Could this be happening to me" were common during the interviews.

T was a notable exception to all of the reactions. She stated that her husband had "made my life a nightmare." She wanted to be free of her marriage and had developed the courage to accomplish that over a period of several years. Her only apparent difficulty came with the anticipation of continued harassment by her husband which was well founded. She said, "I was afraid of what the consequences would be (and they were) just what I was afraid of."

Financial concerns. G, L and U had semi-skilled jobs at the time of the divorce and they were primarily concerned about how they would be able to support their children. G said, "How could I support them?" L said, "The initial shock was financial." U said "I knew I could support myself, but I didn't think I could give (son) all the things he should have."

M and J were not employed. Their concern was immediate. M had no food at one point and said, "Where in the heck was the money coming from to feed my kids?" J was concerned about getting enough money to leave her husband and fly home. She said, "My first thought was, 'Who's going to give me the money to fly out of here?'"

T was unusual in that she had a good paying job at the time of the divorce but lost it shortly after. Her firing was due to harassment by her husband while she was on the job.

Four of the women found it necessary to go on welfare after the divorce. The experience of having to go on welfare was humiliating for them but necessary for survival. T said, "I'll go right to the bottom, you don't have to push." L said, "I was fired and then I went on food stamps." M said, "Welfare's like no money at all." J said, "I hated to go down there in the first place and then have to fight with those people at welfare." G did not go on welfare because her husband agreed to support her until she was able to support herself. In addition to going on welfare, L, M and J were further humiliated by having to petition the courts for child support.

M summed up the plight of the welfare mother with, "As far as food and clothing go, my family helps a lot, but to come up with some of the extra money to go to Kennywood, or to the movies or McDonald's... All the things you want to give your kids and can't."

Single parenting. All of the women expressed fear related to being a single parent. They discussed the total responsibility of the care giving and perceived that care as being two-fold—emotional and financial. The children of L, M and U suffered from what they perceived as symptoms of maladjustment. L said, "I worried about my youngest. He started to become a behavior problem in school." M said, "He (son) was a bully and my daughter, she started to stutter." U said, "He doesn't talk right." All of the women stated that they saw the problems as a result of lack of interest in the children by their husbands. However, M and U also discussed that they had abused their children during the divorce process when they were under stress. U said, "I feel lousy as a parent. I felt bad about that." However, with the exception of U, none of the women voiced feeling inadequate as a parent.

T expressed the need for a break. She said, "It's not a break from the kid. It's a break from the responsibility." T explained that she always worried about her daughter when she left the child with a baby sitter.

J was pregnant at the time of the divorce. Her reason for leaving her husband was due to his insistence that she get an abortion. An abortion was unacceptable to J, but she entertained the option of placing her daughter up for adoption. She said, "It took me 'til then (the day of delivery) to decide. I kept her." She said, "I read a lot about single parenting, and I thought if they can do it so can I."

Interpersonal concerns. Interpersonal concerns emerged as least important of all the concerns for the women in this group. They indicated why in two ways. G, L and J said they didn't have time to think about dating. They were too busy thinking about their financial and single parenting problems. G said, "I didn't think about it. I was too busy." L said, "I just wanted to get through each day." J said, "There wasn't any social life. I had to stay home and watch my daughter." A second pattern was discussed concerning the way some of the women felt about men. L, U and T expressed a deep distrust for men with, "I never let myself all the way out," and "I thought I would never be able to trust men again."

Both T and M explained that they socialized shortly after the divorce, but felt uncomfortable with the sexual demands they felt were made on them. M said, "Men only want one thing, and it's not for me. So I quit."

Self-esteem. Among working class women, the discussion of self-esteem did not surface during the part of the interview devoted to the pre-divorce experience of marriage. The discussion of self-esteem only appears in the discussion of the emotional reaction to the divorce. Working class women perceived their self-esteem as being a product of their status as a married person. Therefore, as long as they perceived themselves as being involved in a happy marriage, their self-esteem was not in question. In the description of the pre-divorce experience among middle class women, the subject of self-esteem appears because the questioning of feelings of self-esteem among those women was a vital part of their dissatisfaction with the marriage.

In the literature, this theme is included with the emotional reaction to the divorce, but data from this study indicates that self-esteem, at the time of the divorce, is significant enough to be placed in a separate category. All of the women in this study suffered from a lack of self-esteem in varying degrees of intensity.

Those women who felt they had been rejected by their husbands had the most intense reactions. L commented, "He always put me down." M felt she wasn't attractive enough to compete with her husband's lover. She said, "She was skinny and pretty. How could I compete?" G and J both stated that "I didn't feel good about me."

T and U, who had been abused, T sexually and U physically, stated they had developed a low self-esteem due to that abuse. U said, "The physical would heal, but the verbal would stick and my self-confidence lowered." It is interesting to note that T did not label her husband's sexual behavior as physical abuse even though it had been pointed out to her by her doctor.

Establishing a relationship with ex-husband. For all the women in this group, this theme emerged sometime between the divorce and the time of the interview and, at the time of the interview was generally unresolved. This theme is seen as a function of a divorce process in which children are involved, creating a situation in which the divorced woman always has a connection with the ex-husband.

The women in this group experienced difficulty in establishing these relationships for different reasons. L stated not understanding with, "I'm still trying to understand the divorce. He completely turned his back on me. I actually feel sorry for him." M regrets the divorce and fantasizes about it, "Maybe it could have worked out if it (a divorce) were harder to get. I would like to see us straighten some of this out. Maybe after I graduate, I could move where he is so that the kids could have a father." U sought revenge with, "I'm staying there (with in-laws) just to be an irritation to him (husband). I think I came back to be a thorn in his side, and it's working." J wished she and her husband could get back together with, "He came to the house. I was a little joyed at seeing him. I was sorry to see him go. I hoped he'd call and come back, but he didn't." T was still dealing with harassment from her husband and said, "Very shaky. He can't let go of me."

G was unusual in this group in that she had established a satisfactory relationship with her ex-husband. She said, "I can talk to him now without hating him." She also stated that she sees him quite often when he comes to pick up the children.

Another area of difficulty for the women in this group is the lack of interest taken by their ex-husbands in the children. G, the exception again, stated that her ex-husband had contact with his children, but each of the others complain that there is either no contact at all or the women wish there was more.

It became clear, from this general description, that a relationship was beginning to develop between the level of involvement and the emergence of central themes. A second relationship was also seen as developing, that of the connection between the traditional value system of the working class marriage and emergence of central themes. These relationship will be discussed in detail in chapter 5.

General Description of Central Themes Among Middle Class Women

The review of the literature provides a comprehensive view of the expected emergence of central themes among middle class women. However, as in the case of working class women, two themes emerged that were not described in the literature.

One theme, again, had to do with feelings of low self-esteem at the time of the divorce, and the other pertained to the establishment of a new relationship with the ex-husband. Categories were provided for each of these themes in the general description.

Intrapersonal concerns—emotional reaction. As discussed in the description of pre-divorce conditions, the women experienced feelings of low self-esteem during the marriage. Those women who voiced having come into the marriage with feelings of low self-esteem which were increased through interaction with their husbands also experienced high levels of intensity in their emotional reaction to the divorce. G, who perceived her husband as more adequate than she, and, in retrospect, felt she was dependent on him, said, "My life was hanging by a thread. I was rigid. I was numb." Of her feelings of inadequacy, R said, "I thought I was lucky to have gotten married in the first place." At the time of the divorce, she stated that she became suicidal with, "I thought about committing suicide." E also expressed, "I want to be dead." Feeling that she had accomplished her full potential by marrying well, E's rejection of the situation was physical as well as emotional—"I vomited. Your whole body rejects it."

It is interesting to note that among middle class marriages, there was little relationship between who initiated the divorce and the emotional reaction. G, R and E initiated their divorces, but T, who did not initiate the divorce, also had an intense reaction to the divorce. She described herself as being, "clinically depressed." T also felt rejected by her husband and said, "It was humiliating. I felt like a circus animal. I thought if I just did the right thing he would want to be here."

In contrast, S, who experienced low self-esteem only during the marriage voiced fear with, "very ambivalent and frightened of what it would be like." While J, who had not experienced a feeling of low self-esteem prior to or during the marriage simply said, "Well, that was a relief (telling her husband she was going to leave)." These two women also initiated their divorces.

All of the women in this group sought personal counseling prior to the divorce and continued in the counseling during and after the divorce. Only S and T engaged in marriage counseling in an attempt to salvage their marriages. Both, however, went into personal counseling after the divorce. These women credited the counseling with helping them come to realize the origins of their unhappiness with the exception of J. J was not unhappy but felt she would need support later with, "I knew I was heading for a crash."

Still another reaction by the women was fear. In some cases, the fear was amorphous as R said, "I was afraid, just afraid." T shared this type of fear with, "A real separation anxiety, a real depression." In other cases, the fear was more recognizable as S discussed, "... I was afraid of what it would be like," and as G stated, "I got hysterical when I was alone."

A reaction unique to T was a feeling of embarrassment which came in conjunction with her feeling of rejection. She stated, "shame, stigma, and embarrassment at work and socially."

Financial concerns. All of the women in this group were professionally employed at the time of the divorce, with the exception of E who, although not employed, said, "It was a plus that I was highly employable." However, each of the women expressed fear concerning their ability to manage financially, with the exception of J. S illustrated this fear with, "There was a real fear that I wasn't going to be able to make it."

Interestingly, S supported her husband and later her child also from time to time during the marriage.

All of the women, although in some cases they experienced lower standards of living, found themselves able to manage financially shortly after the divorce as E pointed out with, "It quickly developed that everything was going to be O.K. financially."

Single parenting concerns. Single parenting issues were seen by five of the women in the group as being less important than the financial concerns. S, the exception, viewed single parenting as a primary concern and, in addition, saw it as part of the financial issue. She said, "It (financial fears) was clearly a single parenting issue." This union of the two issues developed because she was afraid that she would not be able to support her son and may have to return to her husband. S explained that she had nightmares about having to return because of financial difficulties.

Guilt was a single parenting issue for several of the women. That guilt was related to breaking up the family configuration for their children. G, S and T felt that their children needed a father and a mother for proper growth and development. They saw themselves as the cause for their children not having both and therefore blamed themselves for the difficulty they anticipated their children would face in adjusting to the divorce.

Another issue expressed by T and E was that they didn't want to be single parents because they didn't want to be single. T said, "I didn't want it because I didn't want to be single." E said, "I didn't give a damn about myself as a single parent. I only gave a thought to myself as a single person."

J, R and E expressed resentment toward their children. J stated that her resentment occurred prior to the divorce because they needed attention when she wanted to escape from a situation that was making her unhappy. R said, "I resented the attention they needed at a time when I needed to be giving attention to myself," a thought shared by E, who said, "as if I super loved him and could not stand him being around."

The women in this group, although not directly stating so, gave the impression that the children seemed to require tremendous amounts of energy both physical and emotional. Some of the energy, however, was involved in worrying about how well the children would adjust. T saw her child being hurt with, "I didn't want to hurt my child." S shared her concern with, "I was really concerned about (son)."

A feeling of inadequacy as a parent was not prevalent in this group, but G and J stated that they felt inadequate. They both became involved in co-custody arrangements as well. They each explained that there were two reasons why they made this arrangement: (1) financially, they felt the children would be better off; (2) they were both involved in relationships with other women and feared that in an anticipated custody battle that they would be labeled as unfit mothers and lose the children entirely. To avoid the custody battle and a discussion of their relationships, they chose to compromise.

Interpersonal concerns. Interpersonal concerns were generally of less importance to most of the women than the emotional reaction, financial concerns and single parenting concerns.

G and J were involved in new relationships at the time of the divorce. G said, "I didn't have any concerns about being single again because I wasn't single." J said, "I just fell head over heels in love."

With the exception of G and J, each of the other women perceived their singleness in diverse ways. T, for instance, "did not give up my social life." She saw her relationships with men to be a function of her attractiveness and saw that as positive. T discussed difficulties in the beginning with, "beginning to deal with my social skills," and "acting like an adolescent with men." She became angry when she perceived herself as being treated like a sex object. She said, "I had to sift out the garbage."

Withdrawal was a coping mechanism used by S and R. S felt that she, "didn't cope well," and "withdrew for a long time." R had a similar withdrawal reaction, but also voiced profound regret with, "I had to accept that I was going to be alone for the rest of my life and learn to live with it."

E, on the other hand, expressed her need for a new relationship immediately. She said, "My first reaction was, "Who am I going to sleep with?" She saw the establishment of a new relationship as a primary concern. She also said, "I had never not been in an intimate relationship." She perceived a relationship as being an important part of her life.

Self-esteem. All of the women in this group, with the exception of J, perceived themselves as having severe feelings of low self-esteem at the time of the divorce. J simply said, "I felt great."

G and S both found some satisfaction in their work. G said, "The only thing I could do well was my work." S said, "I saw myself as being somewhat successful at work." However, outside of the work situation, they did not value themselves.

T stated, "I did not value myself." Her reaction, however, did not reach the intensity of that of R and E. Both of these women entertained thoughts of suicide. R said, "I thought I was ugly, fat, old and that I couldn't compete on the market very well. I felt like giving up." E said, "Like shit. I felt ugly, I felt stupid. Like my life was over. I wanted to die."

Establishing a relationship with ex-husband. The difficulty with establishing a relationship is related to the similarities between how the women perceived themselves being treated in the marriage and how they perceive themselves as being treated after the divorce. The treatment is, as the women perceived it, a manifestation of how valued they were as a spouse and now as a person. The feeling of not being valued as a person after the divorce by their ex-husbands promoted resentment on the part of the women and a concerted effort, in some cases, to be more assertive with their ex-spouses.

T stated directly that she, "would have to be more assertive with him." She explained that he still tries to put her down. E said, "There's some antagonism associated with (son)," but E perceived that antagonism as a way of him trying to control her life. R said, "He uses money to get at me. I'm having a lot of trouble with him right now."

G, on the other hand, received positive reinforcement from her ex-husband for personal growth before and after the divorce. G said, "He said he could see all the things I see now when we were married, but I couldn't see it." J received support from her husband during the marriage and says of him, "The poor guy is so sweet, but he still thinks he failed. He still cares about me so the issue can never be resolved."

As in the case of the working class women, a relationship between the egalitarian values of the middle class marriage and the emergence of central themes was beginning to develop. However, there did not appear to be a noticeable relationship between the level of involvement in the marriage and the emergence of a central theme. The lack of relationship in this area may be due to the limited population sample in conjunction with the observation that each of the women in this group were highly involved in their marriage.

Although a relationship between level of involvement cannot be seen, a relationship between the level of feelings of inadequacy during the marriage and the intensity of the emotional reaction was revealed in this general description. The two relationships will be discussed in detail in chapter 5.

General Description of the Resolution of Central Themes in Post-divorce Adjustment Among Working Class Women

An examination of the data indicates that among working class women, a common process was evident in the resolution of the themes. Women in this group first addressed themselves to the joint problem of financial stability and a stable atmosphere in which to raise their children. Later in the process, they began to adjust emotionally and as a result of that adjustment began to develop a better self-esteem.

One woman in this group, U, has several unresolved themes. The other women have one unresolved theme in common—that of establishing a new relationship with the husband.

Intra-personal concerns—emotional reaction to the divorce. All of the women in this group discussed the first year after the divorce was the most difficult emotionally. G said, "It took time to get over the shock." L said, "I prayed a lot during that time just to get peace of mind and to be able to cope with each day." M said, "It was kind of hard to adjust." J said, "It was hard," and T said, "I spent a year in therapy."

G, L, M and T needed to learn how to make decisions on their own. Making those decisions was difficult for them because they had depended on their husbands to make decisions during the marriage, and they were afraid they would make mistakes.

G said, "There was a need to maintain the independence I was beginning to feel," and she says of herself at the time of the interview, "I can make decisions now." L said, "It became easier, and I became stronger. Each crisis that I went through gave me a feeling of self-satisfaction. That is solved, and I did it myself." She said of herself at the time of the interview, "I found out that I was a much stronger person than I realized." M said, "I started to pick up the pieces and now it's almost together." J said, "So, when I sat down and thought about it, I thought I would be better off." T said, "I did nothing but sit down and figure out how I was going to be perfect. I spent a lot of time thinking."

G, M and J expressed the need for removing themselves from the influence of their families in order to develop or maintain a feeling of independence. G said, "Then I moved ... because I was afraid I would let them influence me too much." M said, "I just had to get out. I'm too independent." J said, "I just want to get another job in a lab and finish school and get the hell out of that house. Anything has to be better than this."

The turning point in adjusting to the divorce came for G, L, M and J when they began to think in terms of the future. G said, "I had to get out before I could begin to stop living that way and start to think of the future and felt that I was right." She said of herself at the time of the interview, "I felt like it was my problem and I solved it." L said, "I didn't enjoy anything; then suddenly the seasons were having meaning for me, and I started to enjoy things." M said, "I started to get in touch with myself and not think about the divorce so much," and at the time of the interview, she said, "When I get out of school and get that job and just have my own home and a car and see that my children have what they want, well that's it. That's what I'm working for."

Both U and T have not resolved the emotional aspect of the divorce experience. They are both in constant antagonistic contact with their husbands. U moved back into the house with her ex-in-laws and ex-husband and says of that situation, "I'm staying just to be an irritation to him. I think I came back just to be a thorn in his side, and it's working." U's main concern at the time of the interview was to "pay back" her ex-husband for damages he inflicted upon her. T, on the other hand, has projected unrealistic goals for herself with, "I did nothing but figure out how I was going to be perfect." T also must deal with constant physical and verbal harassment. She complained of being nervous at the time of the interview and not knowing what was going to happen next.

Financial concerns. Only two of the women in this group, G and L, were involved in property settlements. In both cases, the women were given the house that was co-owned by them or their husbands. G sold her house and used the proceeds to buy another house in another area. L has stayed in her house.

G is unusual in that her husband agreed to support her and her children until she was able to support herself. She said, "He's been giving us quite a lot financially." G eventually qualified for Jobpower and returned to school for a degree in computer programming. At the time of the follow-up interview, G was working as a computer programmer and said, "I feel great about that."

With the exception of G and L, the rest of the women went on welfare after the divorce. L could not qualify because she had a house and a summer cottage. However, L stated that she was destitute after losing her job and her husband's refusal to support her children until after she agreed to the divorce. L eventually got a full-time job and another part-time job. She said of herself at the time of the interview, "Financially, I still have rough spots." In addition, L's husband now gives her child support.

M, T and J were on welfare at the time of the interview but under different circumstances. M has her own apartment in a low income housing project. She said, "The things you want to give your kids and can't." M decided to go back to nursing school in order to support her family. J is living at home with her mother and has gotten a part-time job. J found living at home difficult. She said, "I definitely want to get out of my mother's house. If somebody would give me the money, I would do it tomorrow."

Single parenting. Although initially the women in this group expressed fear as a reaction to being a single parent, each of the women perceived their responsibilities as a parent to be of principal importance. The women tackled the problems using two distinct attitudes. Some of the women perceived themselves and their children as a "we" unit. G used this approach and said, "We talked more. Like we talked all the time," as did L with, "The kids and I learned that the world doesn't stop." The other women saw themselves as "I" and their children as "they, he or her." M described her relationship with "I'm just more at ease with myself and they're better for it," and J using the same approach said, "I like raising her now." T discussed the decisions she had to make about her daughter with, "After her, I try to take care of other factors in my life."

U has not resolved her fears about the responsibilities of single parenting nor come to any conclusions about child rearing methods. She discussed aspects of the responsibility of her son that she didn't like with, "As a parent, I despise playing the father role." U feels inadequate as a parent and is concerned now about her son's negative behavior which she feels is a result of him having watched her being beaten. She herself has abused her child and reacts by, "I scream a lot because I have put black and blue marks on him, and that scares me because I think I'm abusing him." U stated that she is not affectionate with, "As far as affection or attention goes, it's hard sometimes for me to give it to (son)."

Two of the women sought counseling for themselves and their children. Both T and M felt that the experience helped them to help their children cope with the difficulties of the divorce. M expressed great appreciation with, "Thank God that help was there."

Several of the women have come to the realization that there is a direct relationship between their adjustment to the divorce and their children's adjustment. As G stated, "I think my kids are better off and I imagine it's just because I'm happier." M concurred with, "I'm just more at ease with myself, and they're better for it."

J is unique in this group in that her baby was born after she had left her husband. During the first months after her daughter's birth, she "didn't have time to enjoy her because I had 9 million people telling me what to do," but she went on, "I like raising her now." J's biggest problem was finding an adequate baby sitter so that she could go to school.

Interpersonal concerns. Three of the women, L, M and T, described going through a process of going to singles bars and becoming dissatisfied with the temporary relationship they established. Both M and T were disillusioned by the experience and said, "You finally decide you're not going to do it just because you don't want to do it. Then you can establish some kind of peace for yourself." L, on the other hand, said, "I used to have a very good time. I met a lot of people." T and L have established long term intimate relations and find the relationships satisfying. In contrast, M stopped dating because, "Men only want one thing, and it's not for me. I'm discovering that it's not so bad being single."

G described her social life not in terms of a relationship with another man but with "She's a really good friend and she's somebody I can talk to and she shares the responsibility of the house. She's kind of most of the things I would like to be. She's independent and relates well to people, and she's somebody I really admire." G expressed satisfaction with her social life with, "I'm happy about it."

U, on the other hand, has maintained a deep mistrust for men, but she complains, "Like most people, I get lonely now and then." U dates often and is involved in a relationship now but, "There's always that little catch that says don't do it, at least not now."

Self-esteem. During the interview when asked what changes had occurred for them since the divorce, the women immediately addressed themselves to changes in their level of self-esteem. Statements such as, "For the first time in my life, I'm important to me," and "I feel better as a person now" were common.

The women perceived themselves as being stronger and have less need to depend on a male as L stated, "I thought I was a woman who had to depend on a man. I was wrong." In conjunction with feeling less dependent, the women have made decisions about what kind of a relationship they want in the future with, "Both of us are going to have to put in. It's not just going to fall on me."

L described a by-product of independence with, "Personally, I'm becoming too aggressive. I worry about keeping my femininity." However, L also feels that, "I still feel that I have not fulfilled my destiny." L's perception of herself still being in the growing process is shared by other women in the group including M who said, "I'm branching out to do other things, and I'm discovering more of who I am and what I can do than what I was."

The post-divorce adjustment among working class women followed a distinct process of personal growth through the success of solving practical everyday problems. The women in this group began to see themselves as emerging individuals with a separate identity with much improved self-esteem.

General Description of Resolutions of Central Themes in Post-divorce Adjustment Among Middle Class Women

Women in the middle class approached their post-divorce adjustment by reversing situations for themselves that they perceived as being negative in the marriage. This reversal is related to areas in which they had feelings of inadequacy or dissatisfaction in the marriage.

Intrapersonal concerns—emotional reaction to divorce. Among middle class women, the discussion of resolutions gave the general impression that the women had a feeling of accomplishment. This sense of accomplishment was related to what the women recognized as being the cause of difficulty in their marriages. G saw herself competing with her husband for recognition. At the time of the interview, she said, "It's a good feeling to know that I can do it myself and not have to compete for it." J, whose family tradition had been one of "doing the right thing" said, "The decision to act my feelings was the best thing that could have happened to me." T, who had resented her husband's treatment of her as an "attractive accoutrement," said, "I had a chance to work with men. They treated me with respect. That was a break."

The discussion also gave the general impression that the growth which had occurred up to the point of the interview had been as R pointed out, "It's hard work. I'm tired." The emotional pain of personal development after the divorce was illustrated by T with, "I was just trying to make it from day to day, and I was depressed, clinically depressed, with huge amounts of fatigue, but not as much as I had earlier."

Although the women had voiced the difficulty of the growth process and had reported feeling better about themselves, they also pointed out that they were still in the process of growing. As E said, "I think it takes years to get over a divorce. I see myself as still coming out." T concurred with, "I still have to see what those limits are."

In order to facilitate personal growth, the women in this group engaged in counseling after the divorce. In some cases, it was a continuation of a pre-divorce counseling situation, and in others it was started after the divorce. Of her continued counseling, G said, "I had a hard time with the emotional part. I really needed the support of that counselor." R discussed the experience of her post-divorce counseling with, "I was in therapy for a year. He made me come to realize that all the things I was afraid of were things I could make happen for myself."

Although J was in counseling, she started with the idea that she would need support sometime in the future. "I don't know if people go through that, but it's knowing that you're going to be punished one day. I have no idea what it is, but I haven't run into trouble yet."

Positive relationships with other men were also perceived as promoting personal growth for some of the women. Their relationships were seen as positive when the men involved treated the women in ways that they had wished their husbands had behaved. T, for instance, perceived herself as being treated with respect by men she had worked with, while her husband was perceived as not respecting her. R felt she had been rejected as a woman by her husband and stated, "Many of my male friends especially; they showed me how to appreciate myself as a woman by doing just that." E, who wanted to be valued and adored by her husband, described a relationship she had with, "I think that coming out of that painful period was due to the presence of a man. A better man whom I saw as a better man and who adored."

Fear of loneliness was expressed at the time of the divorce, and each woman dealt with that loneliness by involving themselves with friends and family. S said, "I had people to talk to and I wondered what people did who didn't have those kinds of people around." G said, "I learned that I could call people and they could help me over the edge."

Many of the women discussed finding success professionally and as G said, "I got a lot of reinforcement from what I was doing, and it started to get inside me so that I could see that it was internal as well as external. I think it's gone from my job to my personal life." In the same token, E speculated that if and when she was successful professionally, that success would complete a segment of her life.

J was unusual in that she "was convinced that I was on the right track and happy, and nothing could go wrong with my world." At the time of the interview, she said, "Later on I realized that I indeed had gotten myself into a terrible mess, but at the time, I didn't realize what a mess until about a year later." In spite of the "mess," she commented that, "It's so much better than the old life that I think I've succeeded."

Financial concerns. Although all the women in this group either had professions or were "highly employable," financial concerns were of primary importance to them. It became apparent to the women, shortly after the divorce, however, that they would be able to survive financially.

Property settlements allowed the women to become somewhat secure in terms of providing necessities. R pointed out, "I bought a house or at least put a down payment on one. I bought a car." The women pointed out that they experienced a reduced standard of living in spite of the settlements as G stated, "I discovered that I didn't have to live so fancy and it was O.K." In addition to the property settlements, each of the women received child support from their husbands.

Single parenting concerns. Much of the fear of single parenting associated with the divorce was initially related to financial concerns for women in this group. However, as the post-divorce adjustment period progressed, the struggle moved away from the financial area into the budgeting of time between children and careers. The primary object was to establish a system of adequate child care.

Two of the women, G and J, became involved in co-custody arrangements. As J said, "This situation was actually better than anything I had known. I still don't have the drain of being a full-time parent." In addition to taking some of the pressure off parenting responsibility, these two gave two other advantages to the co-custody: (1) The children are financially and emotionally more stable, and (2) the co-custody arrangement avoided a custody battle they thought they would lose because of their relationship with other women.

S and R arranged to live with other people who could relieve some of the pressure. S lived with a friend saying, "After 6 or 8 months on my own, I said well I can't deal with this. I needed some support in terms of child care and needed some help with the rent, so that's the way we worked it out." R arranged to have a student live with her to "take over when I was working."

Both T and E managed by themselves. T found the initial stages of the adjustment period with her son to be exhausting. She arranged a system of child care which required that several people be partially responsible for her son during the day while she worked. She found the daily routine to be exhausting. "I'd finish dinner and collapse, except I couldn't collapse because I still had work to do for my job."

Several of the women gave the impression that their parenting skills had improved as J pointed out, "Now that I have the kids where I want to be, it's much better." G concurred with, "My best experience of parenting was when I was completely on my own."

On the other hand, R expressed a conflict between the need to do "what I want" and "the buck stops with me all the time." She appeared upset during the interview and said, "I've got to stop talking about this. I'm starting to get upset."

R, like T and E, stated, "I don't like being a single parent. The not wanting to be a single parent was related to the expressed desire to marry again. E stated that she knew if she had a permanent relationship with a man and a career she was happy in, "everything will fall into place with my son."

Interpersonal concerns. At the time of the interview, the women in this group had moved through various processes in an attempt to establish intimate relationships. S and R "did the bars." Both of them found that situation unsatisfactory. S said, "I didn't cope well. I withdrew for a while." Both women are at the point now where they want "to have some longer relationships."

In contrast, G and J had been involved in relationships at the time of the divorce and, at the time, found those relationships to be satisfying. G, however, was in the process of re-evaluating the relationship with, "So I may be by myself, and I'm not sure I'll have a partner." J, on the other hand, was still happy with her relationship, but regretted "never had a chance to sit back and think about my sexuality."

In keeping with their strong desire to always be in an intimate relationship, both T and E maintained an active social life. E became involved with, "someone very supportive. Somebody very human." E credits this relationship with "coming out of that painful period." E now wants to "be in a good relationship with a man." In contrast, T found in dating relationships that she was being treated as a "sex object." She resented that and said of future permanent relationships, "I'd have to negotiate, otherwise I'm sacrificing myself to the man again." At the time of the interview, T discussed progress in her career but said, "I had a lot of sadness that I have a career and no relationship." She wasn't sure that she had time for both, but wanted both.

Self-esteem at the time of the interview. A common thread running through the divorce experience among middle class women had been an involvement in activities directed towards professional achievement. This concern for professional achievement manifested itself for some women at specific times in their lives, while for others this concern was constant throughout their lives.

Those women who were more constant in their concern for professional achievement and were highly involved in their careers, gauged their level of post-divorce personal growth on their level of professional achievement.

G, who felt inadequate in the marriage and a less capable person than her husband both professionally and personally, said of herself, "Professionally, I feel very, very good." G also became aware that she "transferred that to my personal life." T also credited her professional accomplishments with greater self-confidence when she said, "I'm a competent person... I can act on my thinking without being afraid of that responsibility and not being afraid of that criticism. Each new experience like that builds my confidence." S, who is a doctoral student, voiced the effect of criticism in the program as being damaging to her self-esteem. She said, "Professionally, I feel satisfied and competent. If I don't have to talk to my advisor, I feel real good about myself."

In contrast, those women who gave the impression of being secure in their level of professional achievement, but less satisfied with themselves personally, addressed themselves to their level of personal satisfaction. J, for instance, perceived herself as "having everything yanked out from under me, all the things that used to be important have been pulled away and changing and living with somebody." In relationship to the feeling of having moved quickly from one segment of her life to another, J said, "I guess I'm regaining strength as a person. I had to go through a whole process of valuing myself." R and E both felt more sure of themselves personally.

Still in reference to personal growth, the women perceived themselves as being in the process of continued development. J referred to personal growth as an ongoing process requiring time, with "I think that's going to take some time." T, in the same token, felt she had accomplished a great deal, "but I don't know the extent of that and I have to find out who I am in terms of that." R simply stated, "I have a lot more work to do on myself."

It became apparent during this general description that women in the middle class were placing priority on their achievements professionally and then transferring the identity and feelings of higher self-esteem from that area to their personal lives. Also, it was evident that many of the practical issues of survival were quickly solved.

The general impression of the post-divorce adjustment among middle class women conveys the sense of emotional rather than behavioral accomplishment. That is to say they are more involved with changes in their feelings rather than in their physical situations.

In summary, the data illustrate apparent differences between the two groups in each of their major areas of the divorce experience. These differences point to the influence of socio-economic factors on the experience of divorce. The differences between the groups and socio-economic implications will be discussed in chapter 5.

Further, the findings have revealed relationships between the values and expectations of the marriage in each class and (1) the establishment of identity, (2) the emergence of central themes and (3) the post-divorce adjustment. The socio-economic implications of the acceptance of particular values will also be discussed in chapter 5.

Still another aspect of the data was the surfacing of substantial unanticipated findings. These findings, such as the emergence of a central theme concerning the need to establish a relationship with the ex-husband will also be discussed in chapter 5.

5

Conclusions

Introduction

The purpose of this study was to generate a description of the divorce experience from the perspective of the divorced working class woman and the divorced middle class woman and to investigate the relationship of socio-economic factors to post-divorce adjustment.

In order to determine the extent of that relationship, insight was sought into the following questions:

1. How do the central themes develop out of the divorce experience among working and middle class women?
2. What differences and/or commonalities exist in the perception of the central themes between working and middle class women?
3. What relationship exists between post-divorce adjustment and the pre-divorce conditions of the marriage?
4. What differences and/or commonalities exist between working and middle class women's perceptions of their post-divorce adjustment?

To gather the data necessary to answer these research questions, tape recorded hour-long interviews were conducted with six working class women and six middle class women. At the time of the interview, each of the twelve Caucasian women were divorced not less than 1-1/2 years and not more than 2, were between the ages of 27 and 33, and had custody of at least one child. During this interview, an open-ended interview approach was used to facilitate a spontaneous account of the following three areas of the divorce experience:

1. The pre-divorce experience of the marriage.
2. The divorce experience.
3. The post-divorce adjustment experience.

Transcriptions of each interview were written and then examined to extract descriptive statements related to the three areas of the divorce experience. Upon completion of the descriptive statements, it was determined that significant data had been missing from the initial interview. Therefore, a follow-up interview was conducted with each subject addressing herself to the specific areas of omission. The follow-up interviews were transcribed and descriptive statements from each were added to the statements from the initial interview to complete the data.

The transcriptions and descriptive statements were then utilized to generate a descriptive summary of each interview to convey a general sense of each subject's experience of divorce. Following the written summaries, general descriptions were developed for the following areas:

1. The working class subjects' perception of the pre-divorce conditions of the marriage;
2. The middle class subjects' perception of the pre-divorce conditions of the marriage;
3. The working class subjects' perception of the central themes of divorce;
4. The middle class subjects' perception of the central themes of divorce;
5. The working class subjects' perception of post-divorce adjustment;
6. The middle class subjects' perception of post-divorce adjustment.

Utilizing the data which has been synthesized in this fashion, this chapter will address itself to answering the research questions. Further discussion will focus on the implications suggested by those answers as they relate to the influence of socio-economic factors in post-divorce adjustment. In conclusion, the implications of this study for the helping professions and suggestions for further study will be covered in this chapter.

Research Questions

A review of the descriptive statements and general descriptions provided information which formed the basis of the development of answers to the research questions.

The first research question pertains to the development of central themes. This question was designed to explore specific ways in which central themes emerged from the experience of each group:

1. How do the central themes develop out of the divorce experience among working and middle class women?

Development of Central Themes Among Working Class Women

Intra-personal concerns—emotional reaction to divorce. In chapter 4, the actual emotional reactions to the divorce were discussed. The variety of reactions experienced by these women, which included fear, guilt, rejection, loneliness, resentment, shock and disappointment, were expected. Weiss (1977), Krantzler (1976) and a discussion in *Women in Transition* (1975) pointed to these reactions as being common by-products of the divorce experience. However, further examination of the literature points to a relationship between the nature of the divorce experience and the working class view of marriage.

Rubin (1976) concluded the working class marriage was based on the traditional authoritarian model in which the conjugal roles were rigidly defined. She stated that the expected role of the husband was to be the decision maker and the provider while the role of the wife was to be homemaker and child care giver. The women in this group, not only accepted and participated in this model, but described themselves as happy in the marriage as long as they perceived their husbands remaining within the boundaries of that expected behavior.

Of the six women in this group, four of them, G, L, M and U, described themselves as happy and highly involved in their marriages. The high level intensity of the emotional reaction to the divorce experienced by these women was related to the degree to which they had been involved in the marriage. Each of these women had highly intense feelings of disbelief and shock when their husbands "broke the rules" of traditional behavior by becoming sexually involved with other women.

As these women progressed through the mourning process described by Kubler-Ross (1969) and Defazio and Klienboet (1975), they recovered from the shock phase. Each of the women moved from the shock phase into a phase which Toomin (1972) and Weiss (1975) described as a depression, including reactions of guilt, shame and a sense of failure. At this point, the world they had created in the traditional mode came "crumbling in" on them. Their sense of failure and rejection was exaggerated by blaming themselves for their husbands' need to find sexual satisfaction outside the marriage.

Still another factor influencing the nature and intensity of the reaction to the divorce was the social importance placed on the marriage by this cultural millieu. McKinley (1964) concluded that working class men and women consider marriage to be a natural rite of passage from adolescence to adulthood. This sense of importance was illustrated by the women asking their husbands to engage in marriage counseling in an effort to salvage the marriage. The husbands refused, leaving the women with a sense of hopelessness.

A third factor influencing the emotional reaction was related to the women's loss of identity with the loss of marriage. Weiss (1975) and Waller (1930) addressed themselves to the loss of identity as a function of the change in environment brought about by the divorce. Interestingly, the environment for these women was "the family" as opposed to "the marriage." When asked to describe what it was like for them to be married, the women often replied with statements such as, "We were a close knit family." A destruction of the marriage then meant a destruction of the family. The roles they had become familiar with as wives and important family members were no longer functional, promoting feelings of devastation and disorientation.

Interesting examples of opposite emotional reactions to the working class divorce were J and T. These two women did not experience the intensity of the reaction felt by the other women. Although they accepted the traditional marriage model, each cited incidents early in the marriage that indicated their husbands had "broken the rules" over a long period of time. J's husband was in debt and was not a good provider, while T's husband habitually abused her sexually. Each of these women described themselves as not being happy in the marriage nor highly involved.

In addition, unlike the other women in the group, neither J or T mentioned loving their husbands, but instead married them for reasons unrelated to romantic involvement. J married because she "was more in love with love than with my husband," and T wanted to escape another relationship. Both of these women left their husbands of their own volition after little or no attempt to salvage the marriage.

Single parenting concerns. Single parenting concerns were placed after emotional concerns in this part of the study because for working class women there was a close relationship between the women's sense of family and their concerns for their children. When discussing concerns they had at the time of the divorce, the women mentioned children directly after statements about the emotional reaction to the divorce.

McKinley (1964) pointed to the relationship between family and children when, in his study, working class women rated their role as parent first, followed by homemaker, wife and then sexual partner last. Komarovsky (1964) also pointed to the relationship between family and children when she concluded that among working class families, the children are seen as a natural extension of the family.

Such comments as "my children were my first concern" were common among these women. Most of that concern was focused on the women's fears that they would be incapable of supplying adequate emotional and financial support for their children.

It was not surprising, in light of the working class woman's perceptions of her roles as mother, that none of the women discussed any doubts about who would be the custodial parent. All of the women in this study naturally assumed they would be the custodial parent. They also did not mention any resistance to that assumption on the part of their husbands.

It is also significant that, despite symptoms of adjustment problems among their children, only one of the women in the group questioned her adequacy as a parent. The women gave the impression that they had anticipated these adjustment problems and voiced concern about their abilities to help their children through them, but again did not question their ability to parent in other ways.

Both U and M abused their children during the period just prior to the divorce. They both expressed guilt concerning the abuse, but only U said, "I feel lousy as a parent."

The literature, which was based primarily on middle class divorced women, discussed a variety of overwhelming problems faced by the single mother, such as fear and feelings of inadequacy (Abeel, 1978 and Bennett, 1978), lack of focus on the parenting role (Abrams, 1978), lack of organization (Kirsh, 1978) and discipline problems (Weiss, 1975). A discussion of these problems was noticeably absent from the working class women's experience, with the exception of M and U.

However, Weiss (1975) reported that children often have a positive effect by providing structure to the mother's life and that women often feel closer to their children after the divorce. The positive effect of children was evident in the child-parent relationship among working class women. In discussing their children, the women used the term "we." The women also gave the impression that they and their children formed a family unit which progressed through the difficulties of the divorce situation together.

Financial concerns. Financial concerns, for working class women, were primarily related to concerns about being able to financially support their children. In most cases, the women had been living in situations which were marginally stable financially That is to say that they had food, shelter and clothing. Two of the women co-own houses with their husbands, but for the most part, there was no accumulation of material assets.

Several of the women reacted to the financial aspect of their lives with comments which connoted present-oriented immediacy. "Where was the food coming from," and "Who's going to give me the money to fly out of here?" were samples of the comments that were made. Waller (1930) pointed out that women with no marketable skills have a difficult time moving on and away from those feelings of immediacy because they have no time to spend on developing new skills.

Weiss (1975) commented on the humiliation of applying for welfare and relying on other people's judgments of the need for assistance. All of the women in this group went on some type of welfare and did experience humiliation in the process. In the same token, *Women in Transition* (1975) discussed the unreliability of child support which sometimes provides another source of income. The women in this group, with the exception of G and T, found it necessary to petition the courts for child support, adding more humiliation and anxiety to their situations.

Interpersonal concerns. Many of the feelings associated with the conflicts of beginning to socialize, mentioned in the literature, were present for working class women. *Women in Transition* (1977) described a feeling of worthlessness which was shared by several members of this group. Further, Weiss (1975) discussed fear of rejection, also shared by members of this group and manifested by statements such as, "I didn't trust men."

Two of the women, M and T, started to socialize immediately after the divorce and became disillusioned with the sexual demands made on them. Kessler (1978) pointed out that a conflict often exists between the need for sexual intimacy on the one hand and guilt associated with sexual activity on the other hand. Both of these women stopped socializing for a period of time following their disillusionment.

Other women in the group avoided the added emotional turmoil of socializing by becoming busy. They stated that they were too busy with children and financial problems to be concerned about their social lives.

Self-esteem at the time of the divorce. Although a feeling of low self-esteem was discussed in the literature in conjunction with interpersonal concerns, the data from this study indicates that this feeling was a major central theme rather than a part of the emotional reaction to the divorce. Among working class women, feelings of low self-esteem accompanied the feelings of rejection experienced at the time of the divorce.

Those women, G, L and M, who experienced intense emotional reaction also experienced intense feelings of low self-esteem. For instance, G stated, "I didn't feel good about me," and M concurred with, "I couldn't hold a match to anything like that. She was skinny and pretty."

On the other hand, U and T described having feelings of low self-esteem as a result of abuse during the marriage. However, they did not discuss having feelings of low self-esteem at the time of the divorce. J also did not mention feelings of low self-esteem during the marriage nor after the divorce.

Development of Central Themes Among Middle Class Women

Intra-personal concerns—emotional reaction to divorce. As mentioned in chapter 4, the women in this group also experienced a variety of emotional reactions. However, the reactions were seen as a function of the low self-esteem with which many of the women entered the marriage. The women in this group, in addition to having feelings of low self-esteem, generally expected to participate in a marriage characterized by egalitarianism. For most of the women, the realization that "something was wrong" came very early in the marriage. That "something" was generally attributed to a dissatisfaction with themselves and lack of equality in the marriage.

Conclusions   103

At the time of the divorce, the women described symptoms of mourning as described by Kubler-Ross (1969) and Hunt and Hunt (1977) such as numbness and depression; noticeably missing from their reactions were shock, rage, bitterness and rejection. There is an apparent relationship between the lack of these symptoms and the women being the initiators of the divorce. Also, much of the energy of the numbness and depression was directed toward their own feelings of low self-esteem for which they generally did not "blame" their husbands.

By the same token, Krantzler (1976) discussed fear in relationship to the uncertainty of the future as an emotional reaction. This fear was shared by all the members of this group. S, for instance, commented, "I was afraid of what it would be like."

In contrast to Weiss (1975), who discussed the loss of identity through the divorce, these women gave the impression that they had lost their identity through the marriage. The study also suggested that for some women, identity was not lost through the marriage, but the opportunity to develop an identity was blocked by the marriage. For example, R commented, "I found out how much I lost by getting married right out of college."

Loneliness was another reaction mentioned by some of the women. This sense of loneliness was often projected into the future in that these women feared they would be lonely forever. However, this projected loneliness was not a situation caused by the divorce as much as it was another by-product of feelings of low self-esteem.

T is an exception in this case because her husband initiated the divorce. Consequently, T experienced feelings of rejection, a sense of failure and bitterness not experienced by the other women. T's divorce experience is more closely aligned with the working class experience in that she came out of a traditional background which she stated was "transferred to her marriage." The implications of T's background will be discussed further in the study.

Financial concerns. It was pointed out by a discussion in *Women in Transition* (1975) that women with professional status would not experience difficulty in adjusting financially. Therefore, it was expected the women in this group would not voice extensive financial fears. However, at the time of the divorce, these women considered finances a major concern. It only became apparent to them shortly after the divorce that they would be able to manage.

Krantzler (1976) predicted a reduced standard of living as a result of a divorce and most of these women had that experience. Krantzler (1976) further predicted that this reduced standard of living would be humiliating and create fear. In contrast to Krantzler's prediction, these women stated that they "found out I didn't have to live so fancy, and it was O.K."

Further, the discussion by Hunt and Hunt (1977) concerning the added burden of getting a job and the inevitable baby sitters was not a problem these women faced. They had already been working and satisfactorily dealt with the baby sitting problem at the time of the divorce.

Single parenting concerns. The problems of single parenting as described by Abrams (1978) included a discussion of the "active bleeding" stage during which the mother is unable to focus on her parenting responsibilities. The women in this group followed the pattern described by Abrams (1978) in that they voiced feelings of resentment toward their children for needing attention at the time of the divorce.

Abrams (1978) also mentioned guilt feelings preceding an attempt on the part of the women to be "super moms." Women in this group expressed the guilt that Abrams (1978) described. However, their guilt came from "breaking up the family configuration" for their children. Also, the women did not describe super momism in relationship with their children. On the contrary, further guilt developed over their lack of desire to be everything to the child. For example, R said, "I don't feel like going to the park and throwing balls."

The problems of discipline discussed in literature were not expressed as being a major problem for women in this group. Furthermore, problems of combining children and post-marital sexual relationships also described in the literature were not part of the reported experience of these women.

Interpersonal concerns. Weiss (1977) and Krantzler (1977) describe a post-divorce situation in which women face a conflict between wanting the intimacy of a new relationship on the one hand and fearing rejection on the other. Bohannon (1968) pointed out that this conflict often results in loneliness and desperation. Two of the women in this group, S and R, expressed the loneliness and desperation of that conflict. They coped with it by withdrawing. R commented, "I knew I was going to be alone for the rest of my life."

On the other hand, Goode (1930) offered an explanation for T and E who became sexually active shortly after the divorce. He explained that the divorced woman needs to reaffirm her sexuality. Goode (1930) went on to say that these women have difficulty dealing with the negative reactions of their children to their sexual activity. T and E did not experience difficulty with their children.

G and J were involved in intimate relationships at the time of the divorce. They were more concerned about the impact of those lesbian relationships on their lives in general than they were with affirming their sexuality.

The preceding discussions were examined to develop an answer to the second research question:

2. What differences and/or commonalities exist in the perception of the central themes between working and middle class women?

This research question was designed to investigate the existence of differences between the two groups of women in reference to the perception of the central themes of divorce. Further, it was designed to explore the existence of commonalities as well. The study indicated that commonalities exist in the reporting of the central themes, including feelings of low self-esteem at the time of the divorce and the need to establish a relationship with the ex-husband; however, differences were seen in the way the two groups of women experienced those themes.

Intra-personal concerns—emotional reaction to the divorce. Kubler-Ross (1969) explained that mourning followed any loss and that divorce constituted a loss of a marriage. The women in both groups mourned the loss of their marriages with some shared reactions and with some reactions which were particular to their socio-economic group.

Women in both groups, for example, experienced loneliness, fear of the future and guilt. However, within these shared reactions, there was a significant perceptual difference between the two groups in regard to guilt. On the one hand, women in the working class felt guilty and blamed themselves for their husbands' infidelities, while, on the other hand, middle class women who, in contrast to the working class women, were the initiators of their divorces, felt guilty about breaking up the family configuration. The reactions of loneliness and fear, however, were equally as intense for women in both groups.

Reactions, particularly for the working class women, were shock, feelings of rejection and a sense of failure. The inclusion of these reactions points to circumstances of the divorce also particular to these women—that of having been told by their husbands that they were sexually involved with other women and wished the divorce in order to continue that relationship. These reactions were noticeably absent from the experience of the middle class women.

Another area of similarity between the two classes was marked feelings of low self-esteem characterized by a loss of identity. Again, there were perceptual differences concerning this reaction between the two classes. The working class woman lost her identity following the dissolution of a marriage through which she had attained her identity as a married person. The low self-esteem developed from a realization that she had been to blame for the dissolution of the marriage. The middle class woman, on the other hand, described entering the marriage with feelings of low self-esteem. In contrast to the working class woman, the middle class woman felt her marriage actually inhibited her personal growth and development. The middle class divorce was attributed partially to the need of the woman to develop her potential and establish her identity.

Another noticeable difference between the two classes is in the description of physical symptoms accompanying the trauma of divorce. Although there seems to be no particular relationship between being middle class and having a physical reaction to the divorce, only middle class women went into a description of them. Middle class women spoke of being rigid, fatigued and vomiting.

Still another difference between the two classes came with the importance placed on the two central themes of financial concerns and single parenting concerns. The working class women placed single parenting issues next in importance to the emotional reaction, while middle class women placed financial issues next in importance to the emotional reaction. However, in both classes, these two concerns were perceived, at times, to be overlapping. This overlapping pertained to the women's ability to financially support their children.

Financial concerns. It was expected that women in the working class would have considerable financial difficulties as compared with the women in the middle class, and it can be concluded from this study that they did. In addition, their reaction was emotional and immediate as opposed to the middle class assessment which was matter of fact.

Several of the working class women had no money or job at the time of the divorce and wondered how they would be able to feed their children. In contrast, the middle class women had professional positions; however, some of the women felt the salaries would not be sufficient, while other women in the middle class were concerned about the equitable division of property.

Further emotional involvement was experienced by the working class women when they were forced to apply for welfare. They described the application process as humiliating. Although many of the middle class experienced a reduced standard of living, they did not describe humiliation as a reaction to that reduction.

Still another area of difference was seen in child support by the husbands of both groups. In the working class, the women were confronted with having to petition the courts for support while middle class women received it immediately.

Single parenting issues. With the exception of importance placed on these issues for the two groups of women, the experience of single parenting was somewhat similar for both groups. Women in both groups retained custody of their children except for G and J who were involved in a joint custody arrangement. The use of co-custody, by the middle and not the working class, as an alternative solution to the child care problem seems to be related to two factors: (1) the working class women's role had primarily been that of care giver, while among the middle class it was shared, and (2) the working class women moved away from their husbands to other states, while middle class women tended to stay in the same geographic location.

Women from both groups gave the impression they were comfortable in their parenting roles. Neither group of women described any unmanageable behavior problems. Further, women from both groups described a degree of resentment towards their children. For the working class women, the resentment was manifested by a description of abusive behavior toward their children. Middle class women, on the other hand, stated clearly that they resented the attention the children needed when the women were feeling emotionally drained.

Interpersonal concerns. The issue of becoming single again and dating was experienced in many different ways by members of both groups. For instance, two of the women in the middle class were involved in relationships at the time of the divorce, and two women stated clearly that they didn't want to be single and started dating immediately after the divorce. In addition, two women from the middle class described withdrawing out of fear of rejection.

On the other hand, only two working class women started dating but became disillusioned. The other women in the working class described themselves as being too busy with children and financial concerns to start socializing.

The primary commonality between the two groups appeared to be the need for intimacy—fear of rejection conflict described by Weiss (1977). Eight out of the twelve women in this group experienced some type of withdrawal behavior at the time of the divorce. Another commonality is in regard to the absence of any discussion by either group of difficulties encountered between children and the sexually active mother.

The general decriptions of the pre-divorce conditions of the marriage, the general description of the post-divorce resolutions of central themes, and the data charts were reviewed to develop an answer to the following research question:

3. What relationship exists between the post-divorce adjustment and the pre-divorce conditions of the marriage?

In order to reach a conclusion concerning the existence of a relationship between post-divorce adjustment and pre-divorce conditions among women in this study, an attempt was made to determine the level of involvement in the marriage. This determination was made by ascertaining the number and/or the quality of the descriptive statements made concerning their pre-divorce experience of the marriage. Also a review of the transcribed interview gave a general sense of the subject's involvement in the marriage, and, together with the descriptive statements, formed the basis of that determination.

Goode (1930) and Bohannon (1968) concluded that the middle class women in their studies who were highly involved in the pre-divorce conditions of their marriages had a higher degree of adjustment in the post-divorce period than middle class women who were not highly involved. In this study, eight of the twelve women from both groups were seen as being well adjusted in most areas and were also highly involved in their marriages. However, the other four women's experience did not establish any pattern. Although there were eight women who followed the pattern discussed by Goode (1930) and Bohannon (1968), it is felt that the sample population was too small to make definite conclusions concerning the effect of involvement in the pre-divorce conditions of the marriage on post-divorce adjustment.

Another pattern, not discussed by Goode (1930) and Bohannon (1968), which was revealed by this study concerned the relationship between the establishment of identity and post-divorce adjustment. The surfacing of this pattern may be a function of a social change which has occurred since the two studies were conducted. These social changes concern the development of individual identity for women, a concept encouraged by the women's movement, challenging the concept of referrant identities for women accomplished through marriage.

In reference to the relationship between the establishment of identity and adjustment in the post-divorce period, nine of the twelve women had established a strong sense of identity and were also seen as being well adjusted. Of the three women who were seen as having several unresolved themes, at the time of the interview, all of them made statements to the effect that they had problems visualizing themselves as individuals outside of the dissolved marriage. For example, R in the middle class had a number of unresolved themes and also made the statement that she "still had a lot of work to do." On the other hand, G in the working class was well adjusted and said of herself, "For once in my life, I'm important to me." Again, the population may not have been large enough to illustrate this point; throughout the study it was apparent that the establishment of an identity was a primary objective in post-divorce adjustment.

Some general descriptions in chapter 4 were examined to develop an answer for the fourth research question:

4. What differences and/or commonalities exist between working and middle class women's perceptions of their post-divorce adjustment?

The literature establishes certain areas in which adjustment occurs during the evolutionary process of resolving the central themes during the post-divorce period. Krantzler (1974) addressed himself to emotional adjustment with the development of a stronger ego identity, a growing sense of independence and the establishment of a satisfactory intimate relationship. Singer (1975) also considered divorce an opportunity for growth and development. Weiss (1975) concluded that the growth experienced by the divorced is developed through the continued effort to establish stability and consistency in their lives.

One of the primary differences between these two groups was apparent in the area of personal growth and development and the establishment of identity. Although women in the middle class perceived individuation as a need in their

Conclusions 109

lives early in their marriages, they had begun to establish professional identity prior to the divorce. They continued to personally develop throughout the post-divorce period and based their judgment of that growth on their professional achievment. The establishment of stability and consistency discussed by Weiss (1975) in reference to personal growth was directed toward maintaining a stable home atmosphere in order to insure the continued advancement of the women in their professional positions.

On the other hand, working class women directed their efforts toward developing stability and consistency in their lives to promote emotional adjustment to the divorce among their children. Working class women discussed solving one family crisis after another and becoming emotionally stronger with each success.

The method used to develop consistency and stability, although somewhat different for each class, established a family pattern conducive to the changed life style of the divorced woman in each class (Mead, 1968). This family pattern, regardless of how it was accomplished, resulted in a decrease in the inherent difficulties of single parenting for women in both classes.

Barry (1978) put forth the notion that in order to maintain a stable atmosphere in the family, two factors must be present: (1) the children must cooperate in the adjustment to the change in lifestyle, and (2) the women must have a sense of determination to succeed. In reference to the first factor, working class women and middle class women differed in their perception of the cooperation of their children. The working class women used the term "we" in relating to the progress of post-divorce adjustment, while the middle class women related what "I did" to ensure stability for their children. Many of the working class women also discussed how their children felt about the divorce, while middle class women did not.

Factor two, a sense of determination to succeed, was a major common characteristic exhibited by women in both groups. Again, regardless of the method employed to generate adjustment, the energy used by both groups was much the same.

Weiss (1975) pointed to another area related to children which was shared by women in both groups. He concluded that children often have a positive effect on the adjustment by providing structure to the mother's life and also that women often feel closer to their children when more of their energy is directed toward the children. The providing of structure by children was a clear point made by women in both groups, especially R and E in the middle class who credited their children with keeping them alive. Women in both groups also discussed being closer to their children, not necessarily because they had more energy to give them, but because the women themselves were happier in their lives.

Krantzer's (1974) second indication of adjustment was a sense of growing independence. This growing sense was described by women in both groups as part of the establishment of identity. However, for some of the women in both classes, independence was a state of mind rather than a financial or emotional reality. A few women in the working class, for instance, were still on welfare at the time of the interview and were trapped by that system. U, in the working class, had not come to accept the divorce and was in the process of "paying him back." T, in the middle class, was still trying to assert herself with her ex-husband, and R saw herself as being manipulated by her ex-husband.

Krantzler's (1974) third indication of adjustment was the establishment of an intimate relationship. *Women in Transition* (1977) agreed, but stated that an intimate relationship can also be not only living together partners, including heterosexual and homosexual relationships, but the option of the single lifestyle as well. Only two of the women were living with someone in an intimate relationship. The others were, for the present, living singly, some with stable dating relationships. All of the women, with the exception of U, had managed to live comfortably with their sexuality and with intimate relationships. U, at the time of the interview, still retained a mistrust of men which inhibited any relationship in which she became involved.

In a new vein, a resolution not mentioned by the literature as being a criterion for adjustment was the resolution of financial concerns. It was apparent from the descriptive statements of the working class women that their financial concerns had not been resolved to their satisfaction. Partial proof of that was their enrolling in community college to upgrade their skills or prepare themselves for more lucrative employment. So, although each of the women discussed their personal growth as being a source of security for them, a sense of not being quite finished financially was a general impression given by the women.

In terms of not being complete, the middle class women, on the other hand, saw their financial situation as satisfactory but discussed having not completely explored their potential personally or professionally. Each of the women perceived themselves as still participating in a growing process.

Still another area not mentioned by the literature as part of the post-divorce adjustment is the establishment of a relationship with the ex-husband. Eleven of the twelve women in the study explained that in some way they were dissatisfied with the relationship at the time of the interview. In some cases, the women wanted more communication with their husbands. Those cases were mostly among working class women who saw their husbands as "turning their backs" on them. In other cases, mostly among the middle class, the quality of the communication was the complaint. The middle class women wanted either an indication from their husbands that they understood the women's decision to divorce or they wanted to be more assertive in that communication. This theme was largely unresolved for the women in both groups of this study. Also, the impression was given that the resolution of this theme would give closure to the divorce experience.

Discussion

Introduction

The intent of this study was to: (1) provide a descriptive account of the divorce experience from the working and middle class perspectives, and (2) to investigate the relationship of socio-economic factors to post-divorce adjustment. It was expected that substantial differences would be found in the experience of divorce between the two socio-economic groups and further that the differences would be related to the differences in the values and expectations of the two groups. The expectations of this study were based on assumptions gleaned from the literature which provided a fragmented picture of the working and middle class experiences of and attitudes toward marriage, family and divorce.

Although emphasis was placed on the working class marriage, Rubin (1976) and Komarovsky (1964) provided comprehensive studies of the values and expectations inherent in the working class marriage as compared to the middle class marriage. Unfortunately, there are no comparable studies of this nature devoted solely to the middle class. In contrast, comprehensive studies on divorce are solely devoted to the middle class with an occasional speculative comparison to the working class. Therefore, this study fills a void left in other studies by describing the total experience of marriage, family and divorce in both groups.

It must be kept in mind, however, that the limited population used for this study was chosen to fulfill the exploratory nature of the study and was designed to be descriptive. Therefore, segments of the population from both groups were not included in the study such as the non-professional middle class women and the working class women who initiated their divorces. A more detailed discussion of these and other populations appear later.

Impact of Values and Expectations on Identity

The comprehensive view of the population in the study promoted the recognition of three significant relationships related to the value system of the marriage. One relationship has to do with the connection between the particular values and expectations adhered to by each class within the marriage and the emergence of central themes. The second relationship pertains to the values and expectations of the marriage and the establishment of identity and finally, the third relates to the establishment of identity in post-divorce adjustment.

In reference to the relationship between the value system of the marriage and the emergence of central themes, the literature indicated that the working class accepts the traditional pattern of marital behavior (Rubin, 1976), while the middle class accepts the egalitarian pattern (Urdry, 1966). For working class women, happiness in the marriage was contingent upon both partners living within the boundaries of the expected behaviors set by the traditional patterns, but unhappiness and emotional turmoil occurred when the husband stepped outside these boundaries. Further, as long as the traditional behaviors were maintained, the women did not question the quality of the relationship within the marriage. The nature and the scope of the emotional reaction, which included shock, resentment, bitterness and rejection, was directly affected by the acceptance of and participation within the traditional pattern.

On the other hand, middle class women accepted the egalitarian pattern of marital relationships. When it became apparent to the women in this group that their husbands did not share their expectations, the women began to question the quality of the relationship in the marriage. Consequently, rather than seeing themselves as happy and then suddenly unhappy, as in the case of working class women, middle class women experienced an increasing awareness of unhappiness in their marriages. This increasing awareness culminated in their initiations of the divorce and the emotional reaction to the divorce experience contained elements of fear, separation anxiety, numbness and pain; it did not include rejection, shock, resentment and rage.

In reference to the second relationship, that of the effect of value and expectations of the marriage on the establishment of identity, the literature discussed the referrant identity of the working class women acquired through marriage. In light of that, it is not surprising that working class women did not mention feelings of self-esteem and lack of identity during discussions of the pre-divorce experience. The working class women also made vain attempts to salvage their marriages through marriage counseling in the hope of maintaining the marriage and their identities. On the other hand, middle class women had not expected to find identity through the marriage. Many of the women in this group felt that their already developing identities had been blocked by the marriage.

In reference to the third relationship, that of the effect of the establishment of identity on post-divorce adjustment, working class women placed strong emphasis on their increasing awareness of their increasing strength and appreciation of themselves as individuals. The women characterized their growing awareness as a frightening and painful but exciting experience. They described themselves as "branching out."

On the other hand, middle class women began to establish their identities professionally during the post-divorce period and transferred those feelings of professional competence to their personal lives.

An explanation of the growing awareness of a need for identity among middle class women was given by Estes (1977) in her study concerning the developmental process of reworking identities among middle class women in their early thirties. Estes (1977) stated that substantial psychological changes occur during this period in a woman's life and that these changes include establishing a new identity and becoming more productive. Both the establishment of an identity and a sense of productivity were seen in the women's professional growth in this study.

Impact of Values and Expectations on Single Parenting

A relationship was found in the study which had to do with the values and expectations of the marriage and the way the women in each class chose to solve the responsibility of single parenting. Working class women, functioning within the traditional pattern, placed their role as child care giver first in importance in the marriage (McKinley, 1964). The women approached single parenting by retaining their role as primary care giver and giving this role their highest priority. In most cases the role was enhanced by the development of closer relations between the mother and her children. In discussions of post-divorce adjustment, the women consistently referred to themselves and their children as "we." The bulk of their energies was expended in establishing a stable and consistent atmosphere for themselves and their children as a family unit. The need to retain the unit as a construct was perceived as a function of the importance of "the family" among the working class women.

On the other hand, middle class women functioning within the egalitarian model, expected and took part in shared child care giving roles with their husbands. It was expected that under these circumstances, the responsibilities of single parenting, rather than the shared responsibilities, would have been overwhelming for the middle class women; however, this was not the case. Instead, it was found that women in this group retained the nature of their pre-divorce parenting roles. The retention of this shared role was possible because there was, unlike the working class experience, consistent contact between the children and their fathers. The middle class women referred to their children as "they" and described their activities as parent in terms of "I". Women in this group tried to reconstruct the family by becoming involved in relationships or by giving that involvement high priority.

There appears to be an inconsistency in both classes pertaining to the establishment of a family unit. It was expected, due to the nature of the working class experience that they would want to re-establish a traditional family unit. However, although they expressed a desire to remarry, they felt they were not ready and wanted "room to breathe." On the other hand, middle class women saw the family construct not as themselves and their children, but in a more traditional fashion wanting full-time partners and father figures for their children. Perhaps this inconsistency is not related to socio-economic grouping, but rather to the changing expectations of women encouraged in the women's movement. It suggests that women who have fully participated in the traditional marriage have found it lacking, and that after having a taste of independence, wanted time to be secure in that independence before negotiating a new marriage. It further suggests that women who expect equality in their marriages may not have had a sufficient historical context from which to draw security in that mode. T, in the middle class, is an illustration of this last point. She came out of a traditionally oriented family and stated that she transferred that orientation to her own marriage. During the marriage, she began to sense that she had no identity and began to build one professionally. At the time of the interview, T regretted that she might not be able to have both a career and a relationship because she wasn't sure how to manage them together, pointing to a lack of historical models.

Impact of Financial Background

Still another finding of this study concerns the impact of the financial situations of the women in this study on their divorce experience. The greatest impact was felt by the working class women. Further stress was added to the emotional turmoil of the divorce when the women had to apply for welfare and were humiliated by the experience. However, for these women, having to go on welfare shattered any illusions they may have had about the security of marriage. The shattered illusions, although painful, gave them impetus to arrange their lives in a fashion to ensure, that in the future, they would be able to support themselves and their families.

Among working class women, the financial concerns also created situations that forced the women to move closer to their families. The move added stress but also forced the women to make important decisions early in the adjustment period. In turn, this decision making experience gave them much needed confidence.

Middle class women, on the other hand, because of their professional commitments, generally stayed in the same geographic location. In many cases, the women experienced reduced standards of living but seemed to be accepting of that. However, the ability to survive financially became a source of confidence for them as well. The women also had a need to maintain their professional status or improve it in order to ensure proper support for themselves and their children.

The study revealed an interesting contrast between the two groups pertaining to the priority of financial concerns. It was expected that middle class women would have little difficulty adjusting financially, but it was not anticipated that they would place a high priority on financial concerns. These women placed financial concerns second in importance to the emotional reaction to divorce. In contrast, working class women placed financial concerns third in importance to their emotional reaction. It is speculated that middle class women may have over-reacted to their financial situations out of fear of the unknown. Previously, each of these women had been supported adequately by their families of origin and then contributed support to the marriage during which they had few financial difficulties and even expected greater financial security in the future. Faced for the first time with having to rely solely on themselves for support, they reacted more to the fear of having this total responsibility perhaps than to the fear of impending poverty.

Working class women, on the other hand, had experienced mild to severe financial difficulties during the marriage and gave the impression that they expected little else. Again faced with financial problems, they put to work options of which they were aware that would offer them temporary support.

Impact of Language

It was expected that the lack of language facility among working class women would interfere with their ability to relate their experience in depth. On the contrary, it was found that the women, with the exception of U and J, described their experience with richness and depth of understanding. In contrast, middle class women gave the impression of being personally introspective and ambivalent about their experience which at times caused confusion and misinterpretation.

However, it was found that language often influenced the way in which experiences were explained by the two groups of women. At times, women from both groups would use the same words, but the words would have different connotations. At other times, women from both groups would use different language to describe the same thing.

For instance, women from both groups described themselves as feeling guilty. Women from the working class were referring to having been to blame for their husbands' sexual relationships with other women, while middle class women were referring to the breaking up of the family configuration for the children.

In the same token, working class women complained of sleeplessness, lack of concentration and crying as a reaction to the divorce, while middle class women used the word depression to describe their reaction. In both cases, the women were having symptoms of depression; however, working class women used behavioral terms while middle class women used psychological terms.

In fact, language influenced the relating of the experience and perhaps the perception of the experience itself. Working class women perceived their experience in terms of behaviors and/or events, while middle class women cognitively evaluated their feelings and described them using psychologically descriptive terms.

To continue, middle class women perceived that solutions to their "depression" could be found in psychological counseling, while working class women perceived solutions to their problems in keeping "busy."

Emergence of Unanticipated Findings

One of the most interesting findings, which was initially unexpected in this study, pertains to the unresolved theme of establishing a new relationship with the ex-husband. Women in both groups shared the inability to communicate on a satisfactory level with their husbands. However, there were differences in how the women in each group perceived this unsatisfactory communication.

Several women in the working class had no communication with their ex-husbands. They expressed a need to re-establish communication and "straighten things out." Some of the women discussed moving closer to their ex-husbands to accomplish the development of a new relationship.

The impression was conveyed by both groups of women that the establishment of a satisfactory relationship with their ex-husbands would put closure on the post-divorce adjustment. However, the ability to establish a satisfactory relationship was seen as a function of identity strength and feelings of high self-esteem.

Another unanticipated finding related to the need to establish post-divorce intimate relationship. It was expected the working class women would have a need to establish a new relationship to regain their identities through a traditional setting, while middle class women were expected to appreciate the freedom to establish their individual identities. However, the reverse was true of the women in this study. Working class women appeared to want to maintain their freedom, while middle class women gave importance to the establishment of an intimate relationship.

Although there were no pre-study expectations relating to who initiated the divorce, a difference was found between the classes in terms of who made the decision. Among working class women, only two women made the decision to divorce and, in both cases, it was due to unaccepted behavior on the part of their husbands. In contrast, five of the six middle class women made the decision to divorce and, in each case, it was due to their growing dissatisfaction with the quality of the marriage relationship.

Still another finding which was not expected related to the importance of identity in the post-divorce adjustment process. It was initially expected that the loss of a familiar environment would promote feelings of loss of identity as well, but that this loss would rank equally with other emotional reactions to the divorce. It was not anticipated that the establishment of identity would have such a disproportionately greater impact on the course of post-divorce adjustment.

It was found in this study that in both classes, when asked how things had changed for them since the divorce, the women addressed themselves to how much better they felt about themselves. Working class women discussed the newness of that feeling, while middle class women discussed their professional accomplishments. Regardless of the kind of identity, personal or professional, the women judged the progress of their post-divorce adjustment on the progress of their identity and self-esteem.

Summary of Central Differences as Developed in the Research Questions

In the discussions of the research questions, two types of differences were developed in the analysis of the data. The first type is the relative difference found between the three areas of the divorce experience and post-divorce adjustment, and the second is the objective difference found between the two groups. Both types will be discussed in this section.

Relative differences—pre-divorce experience. It has been pointed out that the two classes had different values and expectations in the marriage. The working class was traditional in orientation, while the middle class was egalitarian. These two basic differences provided insight into the differing natures of the marriage in each class.

Working class women stated clearly that their husbands made the decisions and took responsibility for providing financially for their families. The women gave the impression of being comfortable with their husbands' position and satisfied with their role as primary care giver and homemaker. They did not question the quality of the relationship with their husbands, have feelings of low self-esteem, or question the development of their identity. The women perceived themselves as happy in the marriage as long as the traditional pattern of behavior was maintained. Further, the women received their identities through the marriage and developed a positive self-concept as a married woman.

The egalitarian expectations of the marriage among the middle class women were not shared by most of the husbands. This lack of shared expectations resulted in the women questioning the quality of the relationship early in the marriage. Women in the middle class did not receive their identities through the marriage. Rather, they felt that the relationship with their husbands blocked the development of their identities. The women described a growing dissatisfaction with the marriage and having feelings of inadequacy during the marriage.

A difference between the two classes surfaced just prior to the divorces. Working class women were, for the most part, shocked into unhappiness by the announced sexual infidelities of their husbands. In most cases, the working class divorces were initiated by the husbands. However, the middle class women initiated their divorces as a culmination of their growing dissatisfaction.

Still another difference found at this point in the marriages pertained to separations. Middle class women separated for up to three years before making the divorce final, while working class women divorced within a matter of months. The separations were seen as financially feasible for the middle class, but not the working class. These separations may also have been a way for the women to test their ability to survive on their own; however, it must be pointed out that many of the women stated that they had no intention of coming back after the separation.

Relative differences—emergence of central themes in the divorce experience. It has been pointed out that the women from both groups discussed the same central themes including the unanticipated themes of self-esteem at the time of the divorce and establishing a relationship with the ex-husband. Another similarity among the two classes concerned the lack of resolution of the last theme. However, differences existed between the two classes in relationship to the way in which the themes emerged.

Working class women experienced shock, rejection, disappointment and disorientation, while middle class women experienced depression and physical reactions. Women in the working class blamed themselves for the divorce, while middle class women did not seem to blame anyone.

The intensity of the emotional reaction was related to the degree of involvement in the working class marriage. The more highly involved the woman was, the more intense the reaction. Among middle class women, the reaction was related to the degree of feelings of inadequacy during the marriage. The more inadequate the woman felt, the more intense the reaction.

The importance placed on financial concerns was also different between the two classes. Middle class women placed financial concerns second in importance to emotional reaction, while working class women placed them third after single parenting concerns.

Single parenting was a frightening situation for women in both groups. However, working class women formed a family unit with their children, while middle class women saw themselves as separate from their children.

Social concerns were seen by working class women to be relatively unimportant as compared to their other responsibilities. On the other hand, middle class women perceived that their lives would take on structure with a mate and felt that establishing intimate relationships were important.

Relative differences—resolutions of central themes. Both groups of women saw the resolution of the emotional reaction as being accomplished over a long period of time. Women in both groups also reported still being in the process of adjusting emotionally.

Working class women, however, perceived adjustment as developing with each problem with which they were able to cope. Middle class women, on the other hand, saw their adjustment developing through their professional achievment. Middle class women also sought counseling as a means of reducing their feelings of inadequacy, while working class women did not.

Resolution of the financial concerns were, for the most part, in the process of being resolved for working class women. Initially, the women went on welfare and some were still on welfare at the time of the interview. Some of the women moved in with their families to solve the immediate problem of food and shelter. Middle class women, however, although placing greater importance on it initially, found quickly after the divorce that they couldn't manage financially on the income from the professional positions they held at the time of the divorce.

Single parenting concerns were resolved for working class women by bringing their children closer to them emotionally with a sharing of the adjusting experience. Working class women also constructed a family unit for themselves and their children.

Middle class women, on the other hand, coped with single life by doing things for and to their children, rather than with their children. Middle class women brought structure to their children's lives and to their own so that they would be able to develop professionally and personally.

Interpersonal concerns were temporarily resolved by the women in the working class by withdrawing from the situation. While middle class women actively sought relationships, however, this theme was somewhat unresolved for some of the middle class women in that they had not established an intimate relationship.

Objective differences. The primary objective difference between the two groups was financial. The working class women became welfare recipients while the middle class women did not. Furthermore, the working class women had difficulty in obtaining child support and middle class women, again, did not.

Another objective difference was evident in the moving of working class women. Most of the working class women in this study moved from one state to another for one of several reasons. Middle class women, on the other hand, stayed in the same geographic location.

Still another objective difference concerned the dissolution of the working class marriage as a result of the sexual choice of the husband. Most of the working class husbands were involved in extra-marital relationships and requested the divorce in order to continue a relationship. However, in the middle class, the marriages were not dissolved because of sexual choice on the part of either the husband or the wife. Although there were other relationships mentioned by the women, they stated clearly that the marriage would have eventually dissolved without the relationship, and that they had been dissatisfied with the marriage for some time.

Finally, a difference was apparent between the two classes in regards to the need to establish an intimate relationship after the divorce. Working class women did not want to establish relationships immediately after the divorce.

Middle class women, on the other hand, perceived the establishment of an intimate relationship as an immediate goal.

The objective differences discussed in this section were typical of the two groups involved in this study. In a larger sample, other objective differences may become apparent.

Implications for Counselors and Recommendations for Further Study

The findings of this study have several implications for counselors. The most important of these is the recognition and understanding of the fundamental differences between these two socio-economic groups as those differences related to the divorce experience. Further, that the understanding of those differences forms the basis for an effective counseling relationship.

For counselors, the recognition and understanding of the differences between the two groups is contingent upon applicable knowledge of the complex relationship within the experience of divorce of the two groups. These complex relationships are a function of the two patterns of values and expectations adhered to in the marriage by each group.

The traditional marriage model, followed by the working class, prepares women in this class to become primary care givers, accept an ascribed identity and to maintain the rigid conjugal roles as defined by the model. In the event of a divorce, women in this class suffer a loss of identity in conjunction with severe financial problems. In an attempt to restore order to their lives, the women retain their role as primary care giver and retain the family construct for themselves and their children. It is necessary for counselors to recognize that, at the time of the divorce, the women in the working class have a need to develop basic survival skills for day-to-day existence. Also, in addition to basic survival, working class women have a need to begin to establish an identity based on their increasing ability to cope satisfactorily with their lives.

When counseling working class women, counselors should be aware of the importance placed on the role of care giver by the working class women. This role and the women's success in it provides structure in their lives and adds to their sense of identity. Counselors should encourage women in respect to their parenting abilities and give them support in their efforts. It is prudent not to change this view of their identity to a more individual identity initially. Among working class women, it was found that the development of their individual identities came with success in parenting first and other areas later on in the process.

On the other hand, the egalitarian model of the middle class marriage creates needs for the middle class women which are different from those of the working class women. The expectation of being an individual within the marriage and being treated not only equally, but as a central character in their husbands' lives, is essential to middle class women. Without the support of the

Conclusions   121

husband for that individuation and centrality, the women develop feelings of inadequacy and experience unhappiness in the marriage. Counselors should be aware of the middle class woman's need to establish her identity as a primary task in the post-adjustment period.

Middle class women also need to adjust to their feelings of guilt associated with breaking up the family configuration for their child. Counselors should be cognizant of the origins of that guilt and guide the women's acceptance of responsibility within the context of the situation, that is to say, they must come to trust their decision to divorce as being right for them in their situation.

Another finding of significance to the counselor is related to the need of middle class women to, as R put it, "come to terms" with their children. Some middle class women resented their children for needing attention at the time of the divorce when they needed to be giving attention to themselves. This resentment was seen as a function of the women's fear of total responsibility for the children in conjunction with feelings of inadequacy as a parent. Counselors need to address themselves to the need for middle class single parents to become aware of those feelings of inadequacy and aid in the development of parenting techniques for these women.

Special attention also must be paid to the middle class women's need to establish an intimate relationship in the post-divorce period. Encouragement and support are required for women facing the conflict of the need for intimacy on the one hand and possible rejection on the other. This is also true of working class women, however, it is not to be an immediate need for working class women where it is immediate for middle class women.

There are two differences between the classes which are necessary for the counselor to be aware of in order to put statements made by the women into proper context. These two differences are related to time orientation and language usage.

The time orientation pertains to the immediacy of the working class women's practical needs, such as financial aid, shelter and food. Working class women often find themselves in humiliating circumstances which can be compounded by a lack of understanding on the part of people in the helping professions. Also, working class women described themselves as being in a state of shock and disoriented. Under these circumstances, women are not capable of generating options for coping with these problems. Counselors can be especially helpful by making them aware of those options.

Conversely, middle class women are past and future oriented. Middle class women have a need to understand the history of their situation and to cognitively evaluate the direction they must take to accomplish what they wish would happen in the future.

The second area, language usage, is an important factor in an understanding of the experience by counselors. As mentioned earlier, women from both groups may use the same language to mean two different things, or they may use different language to mean the same thing. Further, working class women tend to describe situations in behavioral terms, while middle class women tend to be more cognitive. An understanding of both of these factors is beneficial to counselors using active listening as a therapeutic tool. Encouraging the women to talk about emotions, rather than events or a diagnosis, fosters growth.

Finally, a difference was found in the emotional reaction between women who initiated the divorce and those who were the initiators. In this study, generally, the working class divorces were initiated by the husband and the middle class women were the initiators. However, these reactions were not seen as a socio-economic factor, but rather as a function of the specific circumstances of the divorce. Rejection and shock are the basic reactions felt by women who have been divorced. These reactions are not present for women who have initiated the divorce. The feelings of rejection affected many areas of the women's lives with an overwhelming sense of low-esteem. Women in this situation need to be encouraged to realistically evaluate their self-worth.

In conclusion, regardless of the circumstances of the divorce or the socio-economic membership, divorced women are experiencing a process of mourning and change both of which are necessary for the progress of adjustment. Women going through this process should not be moved too quickly toward resolution without first having the cathartic effect of restructuring the total experience of the marriage and the divorce.

A most valuable study, however, would be a follow-up study done 4 or 5 years after the divorce. The purpose of this study would be to compare the perceptions of the subjects at the time of the study with their perceptions much later in the post-divorce adjustment period. It would be particularly interesting to find out how those perceptions have changed, if the subjects had resolved the unresolved conflicts and finally, if there has been any change in their perception of their adjustment.

Other studies should include segments of the population excluded from this study. A parallel study using men as subjects, for instance, would add insight into the divorce experience of men with the advantage of comparing the results across classes.

Another segment of the population appropriate for study is that group of middle class women who were not professionally employed at the time of the divorce and/or who did not have any marketable skills. In the same token, working class women who had careers at the time of the divorce also should be subjects of a study. Both these groups of women provide information related to the importance of identity based on career affiliation for working class women and identity based on family for middle class women in the divorce experience.

Non-custodial mothers and women without children would add valuable information concerning the emergence of central themes and their resolutions under conditions that were not observed in this study. Further value in a study of this nature would be realized in the comparison of the divorce experience of these women to the experience of the custodial parent.

Still other segments of the population include women from racial groups other than white and socio-economic groups other than working or middle class. Studies including these women would substantiate the influence of socio-economic factors in the divorce experience, as well as the cultural influences.

This study also dealt primarily with working class women whose divorces were initiated by their husbands and middle class women who initiated their divorces. A study with working class women who initiated their divorces and middle class women who did not would provide further information pertaining to the effects of the initiation of the divorce on the emotional reaction to the divorce.

Lastly, it is suggested that studies involving each of the central themes and their subsequent resolutions would be of great value. Studies of this nature would provide information about the experience of these themes in depth.

Summary. It was expected that differences between the two groups would be found. This study fulfilled the expectation with a number of significant findings. Some of those findings were clear differences, while others involved complex relationships. However, it has promoted the recognition that divorce is not an event isolated from other events in a person's life, but rather part of a continual flow of events, each impacting on the other. That is to say that divorce must be viewed in context with a person's whole life rather than within the confines of that short period of time.

Appendix A

Biographical Questionnaire

1. First Name _____

2. What is your birthdate? Month _____ Day _____ Year _____

3. How many children do you have? _____

4. Do all of the children live with you? _____

5. If not, how many live with you? _____

6. How long have you been divorced? Years _____ Months _____

7. How old were you when you got married? _____

8. How many years were you married? _____

9. Was this your first marriage? _____

10. Was this your ex-spouse's first marriage? _____

11. What was your occupation at the time of your marriage? _____

12. How many years of education did you have at the time of marriage? _____

13. How many years of education did your husband have at the time of marriage? _____

Your participation in this study is completely voluntary. The information gained from this interview will remain confidential and your identity will not be revealed.

Appendix A

I understand that the interview will be taped, transcribed and analyzed, that the transcripts will be identified by code number, that the interviews will be published, but all identifying marks will be removed, and that the tapes will be erased immediately after the final analysis.

I understand that my participation in this study is voluntary.

Signed _____

Appendix B

Interview 1A

I. What was it like for you to be married?

S. I married my husband because I thought he had all the things I'd always wanted. My parents were divorced; I was raised by grandparents; I had a lot of trouble with my mother; and (husband) came from a Catholic home; and we went to church together; and I thought he cared so much about his parents, but that was one of the attractions. When I first married it was great until his mother decided that she didn't particularly care for me. I think that started our early problems, disillusioning me a bit.

I. Describe to me what you mean by great.

S. I felt secure. Like I had somebody for me. I had an apartment that was mine, that no one was going to whisk me out of or take me away from.

I. What happened with his mother?

S. I thought it was probably just jealousy. She had been the big thing in the family, everything was for her. If she didn't get her way, she'd get migraine headaches; she was really something. Then I was expected to call her every day; she could not call me, I would have to telephone her. If I didn't call her, she'd get on (husband's) father's back and then his father would call (husband) and get on his back, over things as simple as a telephone call. And (husband) was really important. I got tired of it.

I. It was important for him to have good smooth family relationships?

S. Yes. And I had thought it was because he cared so very deeply about them. I came to realize I don't think he really cared much about them at all; I think he was just afraid of them. That was the way he was brought up and that was the expected thing and, besides that, I was 18 when we got married and he was 19, so really young too.

I. And how did that progress from that point on?

S. It never got any better. I was pregnant when we were married and I told my grandmother right away which was really hard for me to do and especially at that time because that was a big thing, and my father and he was to tell his parents, and I thought he had, like he would leave on a weekend on a Saturday, and he'd go over and he'd come home and he'd say well, I told them.

I. (Husband) was to tell his parents?

S. Yes, (husband) was to tell his parents, but I would have gone with (husband) to tell his parents. I told mine on my own. It seems so silly now, but at the time it was such a big thing. But he preferred to go by himself so he would leave and he'd come home and he'd tell me, well, I told them, and it's okay, you don't have to worry any more. Then I'd talk to his mother later on the next day or whatever and realize they had no idea what was going on. He'd lie to me over and over again, just because he was afraid to tell them. But I really don't think that he was afraid of hurting them. I think he was just frightened of them. Finally one time he told them I was pregnant, but he didn't tell them when the baby was due. They assumed probably the baby was due like in November when actually it was going to be born in August. I must have finally believed that he had told them that the baby was going to be born in August. (Husband) and I went to a big family gathering, a birthday party for his grandmother. One of his cousins asked me when the baby was going to be born. I told her in August. She, in the course of the day, took that back to her mother or whatever, the aunt, the mother went to (husband's) mom and told her that the baby was going to be born in August. By that time, the whole family knew about it other than his actual parents, and they were absolutely furious, and I couldn't blame her, you know, I couldn't blame them at all. But at the time, well I never have and I have just never said anything to them about it, and they assume that that was all me trying to keep it from them or whatever, and I never have.

I. Was that the beginning of problems?

S. No, that was just one of the things; we got over that and we were happy. One big thing with me is honesty. I used to tell him I could take just about anything, but I could not take being lied to. It's just against my grain. But we were happy for a number of years.

I. What are some of the things that made you happy about those years?

S. I was happy because, like I told you, my grandmother is so important to me. She had two daughters, my mother and my aunt. My mom has had problems for as long as I can remember. She was divorced when she was very young, married a man who is an alcoholic, divorced him once, had problems with me when I tried to live with them, remarried him again, had a nervous breakdown, went through the shock treatments and the whole thing, but my grandmother had a lot of problems with my mother and then my aunt's marriage had some really hard times, and I thought that I was going to make my grandmother happy and make my sister happy. I was happy myself, but it really pleased me because I thought everyone else thought my marriage was so perfect, and they were getting something out of it. Does that make sense?

I. What I hear you saying is that you had a marriage that you felt was good and it made you happy because it was a satisfying relationship for you and it appeared to be satisfying to everyone else, so they didn't have to worry about you. What are some of the things that made you happy besides satisfying your family?

S. I liked him. I genuinely liked him. He had good points. We enjoyed doing a lot of things together, like camping, being outside, working on the house, we got along well.

I. What are some of the major things that you remember about that particular period in your life, what are some of the highlights of your married life? Or just things that you remember specifically; you mentioned the business with the baby first, and then you mentioned that you enjoyed doing things together. Were there any other major things that you thought about when you were married that were good about the marriage?

S. We got very involved in church. That made me happy, not so much because I developed any great faith, I didn't. I always wanted to though. I would really like to believe wholeheartedly, and I don't. That was something that (husand) and I were both interested in we were doing together. We met a lot of new people through it, and we did a fairly good job so that was important in our life at that time.

130   Appendix B

I. Did you do anything else?

S. Kids made me happy. We lived in a little house that we bought for $13,000 and fixed it just the way we wanted it. We put a lot of time into it and that was enjoyable. I didn't mind housework. I love to cook and still do. Just really simple things at that time made me happy; cooking a big dinner, having my grandmother out, eventually after his parents calmed down a bit entertaining them and having them up.

I. What was it like for you when the marriage started going bad? What was it like when you began to realize that things weren't going right?

S. Well, it started over a problem with sex. I've had bad experiences with my stepfather so I had always been a bit frightened anyway, and I think that maybe (husband) knew that was the one way he could really get to me and hurt me, so our problems started out with sex.

I. How did it hurt you?

S. He'd hit me if I wasn't interested in relations; he'd bite me, leave marks but in places where other people would not see. No one knew that was going on. And it was awful. It was the next morning he'd feel bad, and I think he really did and he'd swear it would never happen again, and I believed that because I wanted to. It just got to the point where it happened more and more frequently, and I was just really crushed. I'd get out of the house and walk at night just to get away; it was a really hard time.

I. Was that the only time that you were abused, over sex?

S. By (husband), yes, that was the only time. And during the day we would get along well, and if we were able to talk, he was backward, shy, and he was just starting out in his profession and every once in a while, he'd have to travel. And we'd work together on that, like I'd coach him; I was more outgoing than (husband), and I'd coach him on things like, please don't be nervous, all you are going to do is meet people, and I thought I was helping him but then these things would happen again. It was strange; it went on for a long time.

I. How long is a long time?

S. Probably about four years.

I. How did you feel about yourself when all of this was going on?

S. I don't remember if I even thought about myself. I must have. I can remember feeling really depressed thinking there just wasn't any way out of it, and I tried to talk to him about going to counseling, and he wouldn't go and I wouldn't go by myself. I didn't feel good about me.

I. How didn't you feel good about you? Describe what that was like.

S. I would feel bad about myself because I allowed myself to get depressed instead of doing something about it, but I didn't think there was anything I could do. Instead of facing this, I said I'd just go out at night and walk and not go anywhere, you know just to get out of the house and away for a little while.

I. And you said you thought there wasn't anything you could do. Can you elaborate on that a little bit or put that in other words?

S. I didn't feel I could tell anybody. The only person I would have been able to talk to would be my grandmother, and yet I couldn't tell her because I felt it would hurt her too much. I was trying to protect her. I just felt like I had two little kids; there wasn't anything I could do. (Subject is crying.)

I. You are really upset about this portion. Describe that to me what that upsetness is all about.

S. I remember what it was like. I remember him intentionally hurting me and I remember being frightened and angry and fighting back, but he was bigger than I was, and it makes me angry now because I think he did it out of jealousy because I was more outgoing, because I got along easier with people. I seemed to have the qualities at that time that (husband) lacked, and I think he was jealous of that and I think that's mainly why he did it. That was one way he knew that he could hurt me, so it still upsets me; it makes me angry.

I. You remember what it felt like to be beaten, to be forced into doing this?

S. Yes, it was humiliating.

I. You said that you felt there wasn't anything you could do.

S. I was probably 23 or 24. I guess I felt that the marriage had been one thing I wanted. I had grown up wanting that, and I made up my mind that I was going to have that home and so I felt like I couldn't leave because that was giving up that dream that I had wanted so badly and besides that I had two little kids. I wasn't skilled in anything; you know, I really didn't have any place to go other than home to my grandmother, and I wouldn't do that to her so I just let her believe that everything was fine.

I. Don't you have a sense of loneliness about all that for you?

S. That wasn't a new feeling to me because I always felt alone. I grew up feeling alone. Any problem I had was mine and that no one else was going to correct it that it was up to me so by the time (husband) and I were having serious problems, I was well planted with that feeling.

I. So loneliness was not an overwhelming thing for you. That particular part of it you were pretty much used to?

S. Yes.

I. After you got over this initial part, you began to see that things were going wrong or you weren't happy with that; then how did it progress?

S. That went on for about four years. One thing that I had always wanted, as I had told you, we bought a small house and fixed it all up, had it the way we wanted it, but one thing I had always wanted was to go back to where my grandmother lived, and so we worked and we saved and we scrounged and we bought a house, the only one we could afford in Rexville, and for a while things got better with the new house, we were busy again, fixing it up and working together. My mother was having her problems as she always did and my sister at that time was 13 and my mom couldn't handle her so she sent her to me and she lived with us for probably about a year. She went back with my mother after we bought this new house. My sister started having problems with her dad, my stepfather, so she left again and she came and lived with us and she stayed for that year when we moved into the house, and my sister was with us; it was really a happy time again. All of us were excited about the house. We were all working on it. I was extremely close to my sister, and I just felt like I was helping her out and things got better with (husband) and me for awhile and again when he would go into these attacks, whatever they were, I'd just keep quiet about it. My sister didn't know what was going on; no one knew and that lasted a while. My sister had a friend that she started bringing over, and I heard about this girl before that she had been heavily into drugs and had problems, so we kind of took her under our wing and thought we would help her, and the whole thing blew up when she told me she had been sleeping with (husband). I asked (husband) about it, and he said that wasn't true, that she had just been making up a story, she was jealous of us because we had this house, we had this relationship and she was just making up the story to damage it or whatever.

I. She wasn't sleeping with him or she was?

S. He said she was not. I later found out he had been sleeping with her. He lied to me again, and that's what really ended it, like my feelings just left. (Subject starts to cry.)

I. What other feelings did you have about yourself, about that situation at that time?

S. I felt sick and bad for all of us, like we should have had so much and worked so hard to get that far, and all the times I asked him to go to counseling and things like that. I guess it was anger too. He could have gone, and he should have had a chance because we really did try hard. So I was angry that any good feelings I had about him at that time were just no longer there. He moved out, and we were separated for about a year. At that time, I started the first office job I'd ever had.

I. What was it like for you when he left?

S. He left; he moved out; it was a good year for me. Well, it's hard. The towns we lived in were about 40 minutes apart. He still had his job. (The tape ran out and the interview continued for a short time before it was discovered.)

I. You were concerned about the responsibilities, the kids and so on. Was there anything else that was important to you in that year? How were you feeling about yourself during that year?

S. I felt better about myself, I think, because I was out working and because I was handling it. I had never considered myself intelligent at all. (Husband) was the one that was intelligent. I had personality. During that year, I found I could work. For some reason, a carpet distributor gave me a job, and it started out to be absolutely nothing, just fix coffee and whatever and then they started training me and I did well at it, and it really made me happy and I was quite surprised and also thrilled because there was something I could do.

I. Do you remember anything else about that year?

S. I remember being tired and emotional; you know, what am I going to do and can remember really feeling badly for the kids.

I. Can you describe that—what it was really like to think what am I going to do?

S. I would think about it and weigh the pros and cons of getting a divorce or staying married. At that time, I still didn't think that I could get a divorce, you know that was something that happened to my mother; she did that, she behaved that way and to me it was failing. I had wanted this marriage, I had gotten myself into it, I had had these two children and I still felt that there was some way I could salvage that, and I was still bound and determined I was going to try. I had more self-confidence during that year because of this job and finding out now that I could do something, but still I wanted both. I still didn't want that marriage to fail.

I. Did you see that as opposite sides that you gaining self-confidence for yourself meant that the marriage would have to fail? Is that what you're saying that those were the two sides of it?

S. No, I'm saying that at that time I started to think that I could have both, that I could do something to start raising my self-confidence but I still was bound and determined there was some way that marriage would work out.

I. Was there ever another side to that? That you had thoughts that the marriage might not work out?

S. During that time?

I. Yes.

S. Yes, I must have. It was just frightening. It had to work for me. I was willing to give up all the years that I had been waiting for that marriage and all the things that I had gone through.

I. When you were thinking that the marriage might not work, what was that like for you?

S. Frightening. Frightening.

I. What were you frightened of?

S. Not being able to make it with my kids. I knew and I know now there was no way I would give those boys up. I thought about how I would take care of them. How would I support them. How would I give them all the things they needed. Being from a broken home and remembering what I had gone through, I knew the boys needed the security of that marriage and two parents. I could not stand the thought of my two boys going through what I had gone through. I needed the security of that marriage, and those boys needed two parents.

I. Is there anything else that you can remember about that time?

S. Oh no, not at the moment.

I. You said he came back after a year, and how was that for you?

S. It was all right. I was really uncomfortable around him. I wasn't very close to him, but I could live with it. I had a job. We had our house and we had our kids. We had dinner together. The things that were still important to... the things that I had wanted. I could live with it. He wasn't quite so violent or at least I think he wasn't (Subject is crying and the interview pauses.)

I. You said you felt uncomfortable around him. Could you describe that?

S. I was frightened of him. I thought he would hit me again or attack me or rape me again.

I. Was there anything else in that? Anything else about that situation that made you feel uncomfortable?

S. No, not really.

I. Did you keep your job after he came back?

S. Yes.

I. You didn't see him as interfering with that or your new found self-confidence?

S. No, because I still had my job and by that time when he came back I did know what I was doing.

I. How did that situation progress?

S. It was O.K. For a while I felt uncomfortable. I got to the point where I saw some good qualities in him. Things were going fairly smooth. My sister was still with us. A few months after that I heard he and my sister arguing. I found out from my sister that he had propositioned her.

I. How did you feel when she told you that?

S. Sick again.

I. What were some of the things you were thinking about then?

S. I was feeling sorry for myself. How could this happen to me? What have I done to deserve this? But that too was a feeling I had had for a long time. Lonely again for as long as I can remember. Stupid, really stupid that I had wasted so much time trying so hard. You know just to be cut down again and sick and disgusted. (Subject starts to cry.) I didn't have any good feelings about it. Disappointed. Thoroughly disappointed in him and in myself.

I. How else did you feel about yourself at that point?

S. I told you, I felt really dumb and sorry for myself because I had put up with that. Disappointed in myself for letting it happen. I couldn't picture myself alone.

I. How could you picture yourself living?

S. I don't know. I didn't picture myself being married either. What would happen to me now? I went to a psychiatrist. That didn't help at all. Nothing came out of that except worrying about how I was going to pay the bill. The only time I was happy was when I went to work. Because for a little while I'd forget about it and I felt like I was important.

I. What actually happened after your sister told you about your husband's behavior in addition to the feelings you were having?

S. I sat down again with him and told him that we had to go to counseling. We can't do it by ourselves and I can't live like this. I didn't want to be like my mother. I'd always been afraid of being like my mother.

I. What does that mean not being like your mother?

S. I do not have, and I try so hard to have, but I don't have good feelings about her. I was always afraid that something would happen and I would be like her.

I. What was she like?

S. She's a whiner and a complainer. She has problem after problem. She dwells on them and tells them to anyone who will listen to her. How rotten her marriage is and how mistreated she is. Just on and on and on. And I think, as I told you, I'm not used to talking about this and it's something I don't do. One of the reasons I was so very quiet about it is I wanted to act just the exact opposite from what you would have acted about it. At that time, when I sat down to talk about my sister, it bothered me all the more. My mom had already had a nervous breakdown and had gone through the shock treatments. I had taken just about all I could take and the old fear came creeping back. What if it does happen to me, and what if I do react like her. What if something snaps and I'm just gone. I don't think I can handle it. I'd talk to him about it and he still just wasn't going. There wasn't anybody who could help us. We could work it out ourselves if we try, etc., etc. I went to the psychiatrist a couple of times and that didn't work. I just couldn't live with him anymore. He left again. He was gone for maybe six months and then we did get the divorce.

I. Did you think at that time that you would not be living with him again?

S. Yes, I had made that decision.

I. What was it like for you to make that decision?

S. By that time I thought it was either my sanity or... I was really frightened that I was at the point that I just couldn't take it anymore. I was more frightened at that point that I would lose it all. I was more frightened of that than I was of living alone. I didn't care if we got the divorce, but I knew that I just could not live with him any more.

I. What was it like for you when you finally decided to get the divorce?

S. I still wasn't 100% sure of myself. I wasn't sure I could go out there and tackle that world.

I. Is there a difference between the fright you spoke of before and the kind of questioning that you were going through at this time?

S. Yes, there was a difference for me. At first, I had been frightened of losing the marriage. Frightened of being on my own, but frightened of giving that up too because it had been so important to me. By the last time that was gone. The marriage was not that important to me. A decision had been made and now I had to figure out how to take care of the kids.

I. Specifically, what kinds of decisions did you have to make at that time and how did you make them?

S. With the divorce itself, or after the divorce?

I. At the time you decided you would never be living with him again.

S. Who would get the house. All of those types of decisions. We sat down and he would let me have this or that. The only decision we didn't discuss was who was going to get the kids. I would have them and that was that.

I. How did you feel about making those kinds of property decisions?

S. I felt I don't like to make decisions, and I didn't feel good about it. I never made decisions on my own. After all, he was a bright man and I left them up to him. I was scared because the decisions were so important and I kept thinking suppose I make a wrong one. I made the decision to get the divorce and that's O.K., but that means other decisions and I thought can I handle that. How was I going to handle the maintenance of the house? How am I going to handle the kids? What am I going to tell them? Can I give them the emotional support they need? I used to sit and think about all the responsibilities, but at the same time I knew I couldn't live like that any more.

I. How did you handle all of those responsibilities?

S. I just lived day by day. I didn't have much choice. The responsibilities were there. Sometimes if there was something I wasn't sure of, I'd call (ex-husband).

I. How did you feel about yourself at this time?

S. I don't remember taking time to think about myself. It was a busy time for me and by that time my family knew. They were all giving me advice and trying to take these responsibilities away from me. I resented it and I still do. I was angry and I handled them by telling them that it was my problem and that I would take care of it. Then I moved, and I moved not because . . . (there is a long pause. Someone comes to the door of the office and asks for something.)

I. Where were we? You said you moved...

S. Yes, because I was afraid I would let them influence me too much. There was a need for me to maintain the independence that I was beginning to feel. It was important to me. It took me so many years to get that. I had spent so many years looking for someone to depend on. When I knew I was going to be on my own, that was it.

I. Was there ever a point for you when you stopped living day to day?

S. No, not until after I left Ohio. When I was there, I never had a chance to live thinking about the future. It took sometime to get over the shock. Other people kept telling me that I couldn't handle it, and I thought maybe they were right some of the time. I had to get out before I could begin to stop living that way and start to think of the future and felt that I was right.

I. Let me go back for one minute. What was it like for you to be single again?

S. I was frightened of being by myself. I didn't think in terms of having a social life.

I. How has it improved?

S. I'm happy about it the way it is.

I. Would you like to get married again?

S. No, well, I shouldn't be so quick, but maybe someday.

I. So you made the decision to move to Pittsburgh. What kinds of things happened?

S. I made the decision, I did move. Then for a while it bothered me. What if I had made the wrong choice? Maybe I should have stayed back there. Maybe I did need all those people to take care of me. Maybe again I was going to fail. There's a possibility. Maybe everyone who is back there thought I couldn't handle it. You know, maybe they're correct and I was wrong. When you're not used to making decisions, it's really tough, and especially when you start out making them with such large ones. That was again a little bit frightening but I still had it in back of my mind that if I was ever going to be pleased with myself, there was something I had to do.

I. What is it that you had to do?

S. I had to get away.

I. When you came to Pittsburgh, what happened to you?

S. When I came to Pittsburgh, this friend that had been talking to me and helping, etc., etc., we moved in together. I worked on the house for a while, started going out looking for jobs very unskilled. I had that little bit of office work in Cleveland, but that was more on customer service; it wasn't typing and things like that that I could really use here, and I decided that oh, another friend told me about Jobpower and thought that I might qualify. I went down and took their test, and I was absolutely amazed that I passed their test, the day had just been bright and I just had the personality, so I was really surprised when I did well on the test. I talked with the counselor there and they had a six week program on dental technician, where they send you to Shadyside and trained you in dental office, and I thought that sounded just great. Well at least I know something. Then the counselor there encouraged me to think about going to college, going to school, but I really didn't think I could do it. I had built up some confidence in myself, but not a lot. So I finally came in and talked to Bill Plumb, and he encouraged me, so I decided to go to school. So I started making some long-range decisions for myself.

I. How do you feel about yourself now?

S. I am pleased with myself. I think I have been through a lot, but I did it; I am making decisions now. I can't believe I am in college. No one ever talked me into a college; I never expected it. There too, starting school; I didn't tell many people in my family that I had started because there was still that fear that I wouldn't be able to do it, and they're going to be right, and instead, I am doing well. I think my kids are better off, and I imagine it's just because I am happy. So I feel good about myself.

I. What about yourself as a parent?

S. I think I'm a good parent. I know I really love my kids and really want them, and I take a lot of time with them because they are very important to me. I talk to them a lot, they talk to me a lot; I am not super mom by any means.

I. What kinds of things are important to you now?

S. For the first time in my life, I'm important to me. The fact that I am doing something is very important to me. Like my grandmother is proud of me and my grades. That's important to me.

I. So you are also getting support from your family for having made a good decision.

S. Oh, yes, that's true. When I first told my father I was going to college, he told me I start a lot of things, but that's no guarantee that you'll finish.

I. Sounds like you're doing some things for yourself?

S. And enjoying it.

I. How do you see yourself in the future?

S. I want to finish school and get a job. Once I have that job I'd like to go back to school and get a B.S. That's my next goal. Sometimes I'm still not sure, but I think everybody feels that way. I can make decisions about the kids without calling (ex-husband). I can talk to him without hating him anymore. That's important to me. I don't like to hate.

I. Can you think of anything else that you would like to say about this?

S. Give me some ideas.

I. No, I don't want to do that because if they are important enough to you, you'll think of them.

S. No, I can't think of anything right now.

I. How did you feel about talking about this?

S. How do I feel now or how did I feel last night? When you first mentioned it, I didn't want to do it. I felt like it was my problem and I solved it, but it was for a good cause. I was terribly nervous when I first came in here. I'm not nervous now.

I. Thank you for sharing this with me.

Follow-up Interview 1A

I. In the first interview you mentioned that the kids made you happy. Can you describe that relationship with them prior to the divorce?

S. I was very close to them, and I feel that I was good to them, but I was very, very nervous all the time and sometimes short of temper. I feel that I'm much better to them now, and I understand them much better now. Our relationship is improved considerably, but it wasn't bad then. I'm closer now, and I'm more honest with them.

I. You saw yourself as being short-tempered with them?

S. I was very nervous and very irritable, and I didn't really abuse them, but I don't think I took the time with them that I should have.

I. Did you resent them at all?

S. I don't think I resented them. I was frightened because they were two more people I had to take care of. That was at the time of the divorce.

I. How about before the divorce?

S. I know I didn't resent them. At that time (husband) was really important, and I wanted them to be close to him. I think maybe I built (husband) up too much to them.

I. What did that do to you?

S. I don't think it did much to me because I didn't have that high of an opinion of myself. I saw myself as secondary. I was caring for them and for him rather than for myself.

I. How do you see your relationship with them now?

S. I see myself caring for them, for all of us.

I. How did you resolve some of the conflicts you had about the worries of single parenting?

S. I started to talk to them more as individuals, and I started to care more about myself, and that affected my relationship with them.

I. How did you see the effect of your feeling better about yourself?

S. We talked more. Like, we talked all the time. We talked about the things that are really important to me—ways that I feel about myself, that I never, well, I thought they were too little. I felt like I had no right to dump my problems on them. Now I feel differently.

I. Did you plan to do that?

S. No. It just sort of came naturally.

I. You mentioned in the interview that you were concerned about giving them emotional and financial support. How did you get to the point where you saw that it was going to be O.K.?

S. I don't think there was any one day when it happened. We just started talking and things started to calm down. It was sort of gradual.

I. You mentioned financial concerns, but very briefly. Can you be more specific about how you saw your financial problems?

S. Well, I thought in the beginning that we would be absolutely destitute. I was really frightened, but (husband) has been good in that respect. He has helped us and helped me go to school. He's been giving us quite a lot financially. Quite a lot is $104 a week.

I. How did you manage to resolve the rest of your financial situation?

S. When we sold the house, the money from that sale was mine and, with that money and with my friendship with Maggy, we bought a house together. I fortunately had the down payment and Maggy makes enough to make the payments on the mortgage. With the money he gives us, it works out O.K. I also went on Jobpower and that helped.

I. You weren't working?

S. No, but I am now. When we were divorced, we agreed that I would get the money for the house, and we also agreed that he would support me and the kids until I could support myself, and I found out about Jobpower. They paid for my schooling and also paid me a minimum wage for the hours I was in school.

I. You have a job now? What kind of a job is it?

S. Yeah. I feel real good about that. I'm a computer operator. It's not bad, and I feel confident that I can support them.

I. What were some of the concerns you had about being single at the time of the divorce?

S. Loneliness and not having anybody to talk to. That was about it. I was so frightened at the time. I was frightened about everything, and I really didn't think about my social life.

I. How did you work that out for yourself?

S. That came with time and with friendships and coming to realize that I wasn't the only divorced person.

I. How did you come to realize that?

S. By talking to people, but to this day I still don't talk much about it. I talked to you because you were writing a paper on it.

I. How did you manage to meet these other people? How did you start to move out?

S. Well, I met some of them through school. My social life isn't all that big actually. It's not that important to me.

I. Why isn't it that important to you?

S. Because I have too many other things to do. I want to know who I am. I want to do a really good job at work and then come home and take care of my kids, and that's really all I have time for.

I. How do you see your relationship with Maggy helping you and supporting you?

S. She's a really good friend and she's somebody I can talk to and she shares the responsibilities of the house. She's kind of most of the things I would like to be. She's independent and relates well to people, and she's somebody I really admire.

I. So you see that as a supportive situation for you?

S. Definitely.

Appendix C

Descriptive Statements Concerning Subject's Perceptions of Pre-divorce Experience of Marriage

Subject 1A

1. I was happy.

2. We enjoyed doing many of the same things together.

3. I genuinely liked him.

4. He sexually abused me. I was frightened of that.

5. He was the brighter one.

6. I felt secure—like I had somebody for me.

7. We were happy for a number of years.

8. I married my husband because I thought he had all the things I'd always wanted.

9. I thought he cared so much about his parents, and they were such a close family, and I cared about him, deeply, but that was one of the attractions.

10. When I was first married, it was great until his mother decided that she didn't particularly care for me. I think that started our early problems, disillusioning me a bit.

11. I had an apartment that was mine, that no one was going to whisk me out of or take me away from.

146 Appendix C

12. I came to realize I don't think he really cared much about them at all. I think he was just afraid of them.

13. I was pregnant when we were married, and I told my grandmother right away which was really hard for me to do... and my father, and he was to tell his parents... He'd say, "Well, I told them."

14. Then I'd talk to his mother the next day and realize they had no idea what was going on.

15. He'd lie to me over and over again just because he was afraid to tell them.

16. I was happy myself, but it really pleased me because I thought everyone else thought my marriage was so perfect and they were getting something out of it.

17. Well, it started over a problem with sex. I've had bad experiences with my stepfather so I had always been a bit frightened anyway, and I think that maybe (husband) knew that was the only way he could really get to me and hurt me, so our problems started out with sex. It got to the point where it happened more and more frequently, and I was just really crushed. I'd get out of the house and walk at night just to get away; it was a really hard time.

18. And during the day we would get along well...

19. I had grown up wanting that, and I made up my mind that I was going to have that home, and so I felt I couldn't leave because that was giving up that dream that I wanted so badly, and, besides that, I had two little kids. I wasn't skilled at anything.

20. You know, I really didn't have any place to go other than home to my grandmother, and I wouldn't do that to her so I just let her believe that everything was fine.

21. We bought a house, the only one we could afford in Rexville, and for a while things got better with the new house. We were busy again, fixing it up and working together.

22. We moved into the house, and my sister was with us. It was a really happy time again.

23. I later found out he had been sleeping with her.

24. He lied to me again, and that's what really ended it, like my feelings just left.

Descriptive Statements Concerning Subject's Perceptions of Pre-divorce Experience of Inner Strengths

Subject 1A

1. I never considered myself intelligent at all.

2. I had personality.

3. I was always afraid something would happen and I would be like her (mother).

4. I didn't feel good about me.

5. I felt alone.

6. I wasn't skilled in anything.

7. I was more outgoing and got along easier with people.

8. I seemed to have the qualities that he was missing.

9. I had more confidence during that year (year of separation prior to divorce) because of this job and finding out now that I could do something, but still wanted both.

Descriptive Statements Concerning Subject's Perceptions of Pre-divorce Experience of Support Systems

Subject 1A

1. I really didn't have any place to go.

2. I didn't feel I could tell anybody.

3. We got very involved in the church.

4. This friend that had been talking to me and helping...

148   Appendix C

5. I felt better about myself, I think, because I was out working and because I was handling it. (During separation prior to divorce.)

6. During that year (of separation) I found out I could work.

7. Then they stated to train me, and I did well at it and it really made me happy, and I was quite surprised and also thrilled because there was something I could do.

Descriptive Statements Concerning Subject's Perceptions of Pre-divorce Experience of Relationship with Husband

Subject 1A

1. We got along well.

2. We enjoyed doing a lot of things together.

3. (Husband) was really important.

4. I liked him; I genuinely liked him.

5. I remember him intentionally hurting me, and I remember being frightened and angry now because I think he did it out of jealousy because I was more outgoing, because I got along easier with people.

6. That was one way he knew that he could hurt me, so it still upsets me, it still makes me angry... it was humiliating.

7. He'd hit me if I wasn't interested in relations; he'd bite me, leave marks but in places where other people couldn't see. No one knew what was going on. It was awful.

8. He had good points.

9. We enjoyed doing a lot of things together like camping, being outside, working on the house; we got along well.

10. The next morning, he'd feel bad and I think he really did and he'd swear it would never happen again, and I believed that because I wanted to.

11. It got to the point where it happened more and more frequently and I was just really crushed.

12. I'd get out of the house and walk at night just to get away. It was a really hard time.

13. And during the day, we would get along well.

14. I later found out he had been sleeping with her (friend of G's sister). He lied to me again and that's what really ended it, like my feelings just left.

Descriptive Statements Concerning Subject's Perceptions of Pre-divorce Experience of Relationship with Child

Subject 1A

1. Kids made me happy.

2. I was very close to them, and I feel that I was good to them, but I was very, very nervous all the time and sometimes short of temper.

3. I was very nervous and very irritable, and I didn't really abuse them, but I don't think I took the time with them that I should have.

4. All that time (husband) was really important, and I wanted them to be close to him.

5. I think maybe I built (husband) up too much to them.

6. I was caring for them for him rather than for myself.

Descriptive Statements Concerning Subject's Perceptions of Pre-divorce Experience of Relationship with In-laws

Subject 1A

1. (Mother-in-law) if she didn't get her way, she'd get migrain headaches.

2. Then I was expected to call her everyday; she could not call me, I would have to telephone her.

150   Appendix C

3. I got tired of it.

4. They assume that that was all me trying to keep it from them (reference to pregnancy prior to marriage.)

5. If I didn't call her, she'd get on (husband's) father's back and then he'd get on (husband's) back over things as simple as a telephone call.

Descriptive Statements Concerning Subject's Perceptions of Pre-divorce Experience of Relationship with Family of Origin

Subject 1A

1. My mom has had problems for as long as I can remember.

2. I had a lot of trouble with my mother.

3. She remarried and had problems with me when I tried to live with them.

4. My parents were divorced.

5. I was raised by my grandmother.

6. The only person I would have been able to talk to would be my grandmother, and yet I couldn't tell her because I felt it would hurt her too much.

7. My grandmother had a lot of problems with my mother, and then my aunt had some really hard times, and I thought I was going to be the one that was going to have this perfect marriage that was going to make grandmother happy and my sister happy.

8. I was happy myself, but it really pleased me because I thought everyone else thought my marriage was so perfect and they were getting something out of it.

Appendix C   151

Descriptive Statements Concerning Subject's Perceptions of Events Resulting in the Decision to Divorce

Subject 1A

1. Well, it started over a problem with sex.
2. I think that maybe (husband) knew that was the one way he could really get to me and hurt me so our problems started out with sex.
3. He'd hit me if I wasn't interested in relations; he'd bite me, leave marks but in places where other people would not see. And it was awful.
4. That went on for about four years.
5. She (friend of subject's sister) told me she had been sleeping with (husband).
6. I later found out he had been sleeping with her.
7. He lied to me again, and that really ended it.
8. (After reconciliation) I was really uncomfortable around him.
9. I was frightened of him. He wasn't as violent or at least I think he wasn't.
10. A few months after that, I heard he and my sister arguing. I found out he had propositioned my sister.
11. I just couldn't live with him anymore. He left again.

Descriptive Statements Concerning Subject's Perceptions of Pre-divorce Experience of Self-esteem

Subject 1A

1. I didn't feel good about me.
2. I would feel bad about myself because I allowed myself to get depressed instead of doing something about it, but I didn't think there was anything I

could do. Instead of facing this, I said I'd just go out at night and walk and not go anywhere, you know, just to get out of the house and away for a little while.

3. I never considered myself intelligent.

4. I don't think it did much to me because I didn't have that high of an opinion of myself.

5. I saw myself as secondary.

Descriptive Statements Concerning Subject's Perceptions of the Central Theme of Intra-personal Concerns—Emotional Reaction to Divorce

Subject 1A

1. It was just frightening.

2. I was feeling sorry for myself.

3. How could this happen to me.

4. What had I done to deserve this.

5. Disappointed. Thoroughly disappointed in him and myself.

6. I felt really dumb and sorry for myself because I had put up with all that.

7. Disappointed in myself for letting it happen.

8. I couldn't picture myself alone.

9. What would happen to me now?

10. I was more frightened that I would lose it all.

11. Frightened of being on my own, but frightened of giving that up too (the marriage).

12. I was scared because the decisions were so important, and I kept thinking suppose I make the wrong one.

13. I just lived day to day.

14. I just couldn't live with him anymore.

15. I wasn't 100% sure of myself.

16. I wasn't sure I could go out there and tackle that world.

17. I was really frightened to the point that I just couldn't take it any more. I was more frightened at that point that I would lose it all. I was more frightened of that than living alone.

18. I felt sick and bad for all of us, like we worked so hard to get that far and all the times I asked him to go to counseling and things like that; I guess it was anger too.

19. So I was angry that any good feelings I had about him at that time were just no longer there.

20. I remember being tired and emotional, you know, what am I going to do and can remember feeling badly for the kids.

21. At that time, I still didn't think I could get a divorce, you know, that was something that happened to my mother; she did that; she behaved that way, and to me it was failing.

22. I still didn't want that marriage to fail.

23. I was scared because the decisions were so important, and I kept thinking suppose I make the wrong one.

24. I made the decision to get the divorce, and that's O.K., but that means other decisions, and I thought can I handle that.

Descriptive Statements Concerning Subject's Perceptions of the Central Theme of Financial Concerns

Subject 1A

1. How was I going to handle the maintenance on the house.

2. How would I support them (two children).

154   Appendix C

3. Well, I thought in the beginning that we would be absolutely destitute.

Descriptive Statements Concerning Subject's Perceptions of the Central Theme of Single Parenting Concerns

Subject 1A

1. Not being able to make it with my kids.
2. I knew and I know now there was no way I would give those boys up.
3. I thought about how I would take care of them.
4. How would I support them.
5. Those boys needed two parents.
6. How would I give them all the things they needed.
7. How am I going to handle the kids.
8. What am I going to tell them.
9. Can I give them the emotional support they need.
10. The decision had been made and now I had to figure out how to take care of the kids.
11. The only decision we didn't discuss was who was going to get the kids. I would have them and that was it.
12. I was frightened because they were two more people I had to take care of.

Descriptive Statements Concerning Subject's Perceptions of the Central Theme of Interpersonal Concerns

Subject 1A

1. Lonely again for as long as I can remember.
2. I couldn't picture myself alone.

3. I was frightened of being by myself. I didn't think in terms of having a social life.

4. Loneliness and not having anybody to talk to.

5. I was frightened about everything, and I really didn't think about my social life.

Descriptive Statements Concerning Subject's Perceptions of Her Self-esteem at the Time of the Divorce

Subject 1A

1. I didn't feel good about me.

2. I wasn't skilled in anything.

3. I never considered myself intelligent at all.

4. I still wasn't 100% sure of myself.

5. I wasn't sure I could go out and tackle that world.

Descriptive Statements Concerning Subject's Perceptions of the Resolution of Intra-Personal Concerns—Emotional Reaction to Divorce in Post-divorce Adjustment

Subject 1A

1. Just lived from day to day.

2. I went to psychiatrist.

3. It took some time to get over the shock.

4. I had to get out before I could begin to stop living that way and start to think of the future and felt that I was right.

5. I can talk to him (ex-husband) without hating him anymore.

6. I can make decisions now.

7. I am doing well.

8. I think my children are better off, and I imagine its just because I am happy.

9. I felt like it was my problem and I solved it.

10. I don't remember taking time to think of myself.

11. They (family) were all giving me advice and trying to take these responsibilities away from me.

12. I resented it and still do.

13. I was angry and I handled them by telling them that it was my problem and I would take care of it.

14. Then I moved... because I was afraid I would let them influence me too much.

15. There was a need for me to maintain the independence I was beginning to feel.

16. It was important to me. It took me so many years to get that.

17. I had spent so many years looking for someone to depend on.

18. When I knew I was going to be on my own, that was it.

19. I had to get out before I could begin to stop living that way and start to think of the future and felt that I was right.

20. I made the decision; I did move (to Pittsburgh).

21. That was again a little bit frightening, but I still had it in the back of my mind that if I was ever going to be pleased with myself, there was something I had to do.

Descriptive Statements Concerning Subject's Perceptions of the Resolution of Financial Concerns in Post-divorce Adjustment

Subject 1A

1. Started going out looking for jobs; very unskilled.

2. So, I decided to go to school.

3. I still had my job and, by the time he came back (after separation prior to divorce), I did know what I was doing.

4. When I came to Pittsburgh, this friend that had been talking to me and helping, we moved in together.

5. I started working on the house for a while, started going out looking for jobs, very unskilled.

6. Another friend told me about Jobpower, and I thought I might qualify. I was really surprised when I did well on the test. Well, at least I knew something.

7. Then the counselor there encouraged me to think about college, going to school, but I really didn't think I could do it.

8. I had built up some confidence in myself, but not a lot.

9. So, I finally came in and talked to Bill Plumb, and he encouraged me, so I decided to go to school.

10. So I started to make some long range decisions for myself.

11. I was really frightened, but (husband) has been good in that respect. He has helped me go to school.

12. He's been giving us quite a lot financially.

13. When we sold the house, the money from that sale was mine, and with that money and with friendship with Maggy, we bought a house together.

14. I had the down payment and Maggy makes enough to make the payments on the mortgage.

15. With the money he gives us, it works out O.K.

16. I also went on Jobpower, and that helped. They paid for my schooling and also paid me a minimum wage for the hours I was in school.

17. When we were divorced, we agreed that I would get the money for the house, and we also agreed that he would support me and the kids until I could support myself, and I found out about Jobpower.

Descriptive Statements Concerning Subject's Perceptions of Relationship with Ex-husband at the Time of the Interview

Subject 1A

1. I can talk to him without hating him.

2. That's important to me. I don't like to hate.

Descriptive Statements Concerning Subject's Perceptions of the Resolution of Interpersonal Concerns in Post-divorce Adjustment

Subject 1A

1. I'm happy about it (social life).

2. No, well I shouldn't be so quick, but maybe someday (in reference to marrying again).

3. That came with time and with friendships and coming to realize that I wasn't the only one.

4. By talking to people, but to this day, I still don't talk much about it.

5. Well, I met some of them (friends) through school.

6. My social life isn't all that big, actually.

7. It's not important to me. Because I have too many other things to do.

8. I want to know who I am. I want to do a really good job at work and then come home and take care of my kids and that's really all I have time for.

9. She's (friend subject lives with) a really good friend, and she's somebody I can talk to, and she shares the responsibility of the house. She's kind of most of the things I would like to be. She's independent and relates well to people, and she's somebody I really admire.

Descriptive Statements Concerning Subject's Perceptions of the Resolution of Single Parenting Concerns in Post-divorce Adjustment

Subject 1A

1. I think I'm a good parent.

2. I know I really love my kids and really want them, and I take a lot of time with them because they are very important to me.

3. I talk to them a lot; they talk to me a lot. I am not super mom by any means.

4. I think my kids are better off, and I imagine it's just because I am happy.

5. I see myself caring for them, for all of us.

6. I started to talk to them more as individuals, and I started to care more about myself, and that affected my relationship with them.

7. We talked more, like we talk all the time.

8. We talk about things that are really important to me—ways that I feel about myself that I never... well, I thought they were too little.

9. I felt like I had no right to dump my problems on them. Now, I feel differently.

10. It just sort of came naturally.

11. I don't think there was any one day when it happened. We just started talking and things started to calm down. It was sort of gradual.

Bibliography

Abeel, Erica. "The Divorced Woman Tries to Juggle Her Many Roles." *Marriage and Divorce Today* **3,** no. 51 (August 7, 1978).
———. *Only When I Laugh.* New York: William Morrow and Company, Inc., 1978.
Abrams, Ellen. "Single Parents Need Help." *Marriage and Divorce Today* 4, no. 9 (October 16, 1978).
A.F.L.-C.I.O. "What Everyone Should Know About Government Spending and Full Employment." Publication No. 53, p. 4.
Andreas, Carol. *Sex and Caste in America.* Englewood Cliffs, New Jersey: Prentice-Hall, Inc. 1971.
Anspach, Donald F. "Kingship and Divorce." *Journal of Marriage and Family* (May 1976) 323-30.
Barry, Ann C. "Successful, Single-Parent Families: Majority Sought Counseling." *Marriage and Divorce Today* **4,** no. 18 (December 1975).
Bennet, Richard. "P.E.T.: New Hope for Single Parents." *Marriage and Divorce Today* **3,** no. 45 (June 29, 1978).
Black, James and Champion, Dean J. *Methods and Issues in Social Research.* New York: John Wiley and Sons, Inc., 1976.
Blumanthal, Monica. "Mental Health Among the Divorced." *Archives of General Psychiatry* **16** (May 1967), 603-08.
Bohannon, Paul, ed. *Divorce and After.* New York: Doubleday and Company, Inc., 1970.
Briscoe, William C., et al. "Divorce and Psychiatric Disease." *Archives of General Psychiatry* **29** (July 1973), 119-25.
Briscoe, William and Smith, James B. "Depression in Bereavement and Divorce: Relationship to Primary Depressive Illness. A study of 128 Subjects." *Archives of General Psychiatry* **32** (April 1975), 439-41.
———. "Psychiatric Illness: Marital Units and Divorce." *The Journal of Nervous and Mental Disease* **158** (1974), 440-45.
Bronfenbrenner, Urie. "Socialization and Social Class Through Time and Space." Readings in Social Psychology, 3rd edition, E. E. Maccoby, T. M. Newcomb, and E. L. Hartley, eds. New York: Henry Holt, 1978, 440-25.
Broom, Leonard and Selznick, Phillip. *Sociology.* New York: Row, Peterson and Company, 1958.
Cavan, Ruth Shonle. *The American Family.* New York: Thoman Crowell Company, 1969.
Centers, Richard. *The Psychology of the Social Classes.* New York: Russell and Russell, 1961.
Cohen, Albert and Hodges, Harold. "Characteristics of the Lower Blue-Collar Class." *Social Problems* **10,** no. 4 (Spring 1965), 303-34.
Defazio, V. J. and Klienbolt, I. "A Note on the Dynamics of Psychotherapy During Marital Dissolution." *Psychotherapy: Theory, Research, and Practice* **12,** no. 1 (Spring 1975), 101-04.
Ernst, Marris L. and Loth, David. *For Better or Worse: A New Approach to Marriage and Divorce.* New York: Harper and Brothers Publishers, 1952.

Estes, Barbara. *A Descriptive Study of the Developmental Phase of Women in their 30's.* Unpublished Dissertation. University of Pittsburgh, 1977.

Giorgi, A. *An Application of Phenomenological Methods in Psychology.* A. Giorgi, C. Fisher, and E. Murray eds. Duquesne Studies on Phenomenological Psychology, II. Pittsburgh, Pa.: Duquesne University Press, 1975.

_____. *Psychology as a Human Science: A Phenomenologically Based Approach.* New York: Harper and Row, 1970.

Goode, William J. *After Divorce.* Glencoe, Ill.: The Free Press, 1956.

Handel, Gerald and Rainwater, Lee. *Family Design: Marital Sexuality, Family Planning, and Family Limitations.* Chicago, Ill.: Aldine Publishing Co., 1964.

Hettlinger, Richard. *Human Sexuality: A Psychosocial Perspective.* Belmont, California: Wadsworth Publishing Company, Inc., 1975.

Hirschfield, Mary. "Anger: A By-Product of Divorce". *Marriage and Divorce Today* 3, no. 40 (May 21, 1978).

Hollingshead, August B. and Redlich, Fredrick. *Social Class and Mental Illness.* New York: John Wiley and Sons, Inc., 1958.

Hunt, Bernice and Hunt, Morton. *The Divorce Experience.* New York: McGraw-Hill Book Company, 1977.

Hunt, Morton. *The World of the Formerly Married.* New York: McGraw-Hill Book Company, 1966.

Hurvitz, Nathan. "The Component of Marital Roles". *Sociology and Social Research* XLV, no. 3 (April 1961), 301-09.

Jacobson, Paul. *American Marriage and Divorce.* New York: Rinehart and Company, Inc., 1959.

Kessler, Sheila. *The American Way of Divorce.* Chicago, Ill.: Nelson-Hall, 1975.

Kirsch, Carol. "Study: Adjustment of Children to Separation and Divorce." *Marriage and Divorce Today,* no. 22 (January 15, 1977).

Klien, Carol. *The Single Parent Experience.* New York: Avon, 1973.

Komarovsky, Mirra. *Blue Collar Marriage.* New York: Random House, Inc., 1964.

Krantzler, Mel. *Creative Divorce: A New Opportunity for Personal Growth.* New York: Signet/New American Library, 1975.

_____. *Learning to Love Again* New York: Thomas Y. Crowell Company, 1977.

Lantz, Herman and Snyder, Eloise. *Marriage: An Examination of the Man-Woman Relationship.* New York: John Wiley and Sons, Inc., 1969.

Lichtenburger, J. P. *Divorce: A Social Interpretation.* New York: McGraw-Hill Book Company, Inc., 1931.

McGinnis, Thomas and Finnigan, Dana. *Open Family and Marriage: A Guide to Personal Growth.* St. Louis, Missouri: C. V. Mosby Co., 1976.

McKenny, Mary. *Divorce: A Selected Annotated Bibliography.* Metuchen, New Jersey: The Scarecrow Press, Inc., 1975.

McKinley, Donald G. *Social Class and Family Life.* New York: The Free Press, 1964.

Miller, S. M. and Russman, Frank. "The Working-Class Subculture: A New View." *Social Problems* IX (Summer 1961), 86-97.

Mindley, Carol. *The Divorced Mother: A Guide to Readjustment.* New York: McGraw-Hill Book Company, 1969.

Napolitane, Catherine with Pellegrino, Victoria. *Living and Loving After Divorce.* New York: Rawson Associates, 1977.

Phillips, Bernard. *Sociology: From Concepts to Practice.* New York: McGraw-Hill Book Company, 1977.

Rainwater, Lee. *Workingman's Wife.* New York: Oceana Publications, 1959.

_____. *Readings in Human Sexuality: Contemporary Perspectives.* Chad Gordon and Gayle Johnson eds. New York: Harper and Row (1976-77).

Rubin, Lillian. *Worlds of Pain* New York: Basic Books, Inc., 1976.

Scanzoni, John. "A Social System Analysis of Dissolved and Existing Marriages." *Journal of Marriage and the Family* (August 1968), 452-61.

Sennett, Richard and Coll, Johnathan. *The Hidden Injuries of Class*. Englewood Cliffs, New Jersey: Prentice-Hall, Inc., 1973.

Sheresky, Norman. *Uncoupling: The Art of Coming Apart*. New York: Viking Press, Inc., 1972.

Singer, Laura. "Divorce and the Single Life: Divorce Development." *Journal of Sex and Marital Theory* 1, no. 3 (Spring 1975), 254-61.

Spicer, Jerry W. and Hampe, Gary D. "Kinship Interaction After Divorce." *Journal of Marriage and Family* (February 1975), 113-19.

Spiegelberg, H. *The Phenomenological Movement*. The Hague: Martinus Nijhoff, 1971.

Suarez, John. "Post Divorce Sexual Involvements." *Marriage and Divorce Today* **4**, no. 3 (September 1978).

Thines, George. *Phenomenology and the Science of Behavior*. London: George Allen and Unwin, 1977.

Toomin, Melvin M. *Social Stratification*. Englewood Cliffs, New Jersey: Prentice-Hall, Inc., 1969.

Udry, Richard. *The Social Context of Marriage*. New York: J. B. Lippincott and Company, 1966.

U.S. Bureau of the Census, U.S. Department of Commerce. Current Population Reports, Series p-20, no. 312, "Marriage, Divorce, Widowhood, and Remarriage by Family Characteristics": June 1975.

Waller, Willard. *The Old Love and the New: Divorce and Readjustment*. New York: Horace Liveright, 1930.

Weiss, Robert. *Marital Separation*. New York: Basic Books, Inc., 1975.

_____. *Women in Transition: A Feminist Handbook on Separation and Divorce*. Linds Backiel, Susan Daily, and Carolyn Washburne, eds. New York: Charles Scribners and Sons, Inc., 1975.

_____. *Women's Survival Manual: A Feminist Handbook on Separation and Divorce*. Philadelphia, Pa.: Women in Transition, Inc., 1972.

Woods, Sister Frances Jerome. *The American Family System*. New York: Harper and Row, 1959.

Yates, Martha. *Coping; A Survival Manual for Women Alone*. Englewood Cliffs, New Jersey: Prentice-Hall Inc., 1973.

Author and Title Index

Abrams, Ellen, 8, 9, 101, 104
Abeel, Erica, 8, 101

Barry, Ann, 12, 109
Bennett, Richard, 9, 101
Black, James, 20, 21
Blumenthal, Monica, 6
Blue Collar Marriage, The, 16
Bohannon, Paul, 6, 11, 104, 107, 108
Bronfenbrenner, Urie, 17
Broom, Leonard, 19

Cavan, Ruth, 18
Champion, Dean, 20, 21
Defazio, V.J., 6, 99
Divorce and After, 12
Divorced Mother, The, 11

Ernst, Marris, 6
Estes, Barbara, 113

Finnegan, Dana, 15, 17

Goode, William, 6, 11, 13, 104, 107, 108

Handel, Gerald, 14, 15
Hettlinger, Richard, 16
Hollingshead, August, 15
Hunt, Bernice, 6, 7, 8, 13, 103
Hunt, Morton, 6, 7, 8, 13, 103
Hurvitz, Nathan, 14

Kessler, Sheila, 9, 15, 102
Kirsh, Carol, 9, 101
Klienboet, I., 6, 99
Komarovsky, Mirra, 2, 3, 17, 100, 111
Krantzler, Mel, 6, 7, 10, 99, 103, 104, 108, 109, 110
Kubler-Ross, Elizabeth, 6, 99, 103, 105

Loth, David, 6

McGinnis, Thomas, 15, 17
McKinley, Donald, 14, 15, 16, 99, 100
Mead, Margaret, 12, 109
Methods and Issues in Social Research, 20
Mindley, Carol, 10, 11

Napolitane, Catherine, 11

Open Family and Marriage, 15

Pellegrino, Victoria, 11
Phillips, Bernard, 19

Rainwater, Lee, 14, 15
Readings in Human Sexuality, 16
Redlich, Fredrick, 15
Rubin, Lillian, 2, 13, 14, 17, 18, 21, 99, 112

Selznick, Phillip, 19
Singer, Laura, 7, 12, 108
Social Class and Family Life, 14

Thines, George, 20
Toomin, Melvin, 6, 99

Udry, Richard, 13, 15, 16, 18, 112

Waller, Willard, 6, 8, 99, 101
Weiss, Robert, 6, 8, 9, 10, 12, 99-104, 107-9
Women in Transition, 6, 7, 11, 12, 99, 101, 102, 103, 110
Women's Survival Manual, 11
Woods, Sister Frances Jerome, 14, 17
Worlds of Pain, 13, 14
World of the Formerly Married, The, 10

Yates, Martha, 7, 10

Subject Index

Abuse
  of children, 81, 90, 101, 107
  of wives, 79, 82, 100
  see children
Accomplishments, 91
Adolescents, 14
  behavior of, 86
  working class, 99
Aggressive behavior, 91
Ambivalence, 76, 84, 115
Anger, 79, 80
  see ex-spouse
Antagonism, 88
Anxiety, 112
  see depression
Assertiveness, 87, 110

Babysitters
  see single parenting, problems of
Battering, 79, 100
  see abuse
Behavioral problems, among children, 106, 107, 115
Behavioral terms, 115, 122
Biographical descriptions, 22-23
  see subjects
Biographical questionnaire, 125-26
Bitterness, 112
Blame, 6
Body Image, 86
Boredom, 73

Careers,
  after divorce, 94
  see professional status
Case studies, 30-65
  see descriptive summaries by subject
Case study,
  definition of, 19-21
Central themes
  definition of, 1-10, 20

description of, 98-110, 118
development of, 98-110, 118
emergence of, 83
unresolved, 108
see emotion reaction; financial concerns; interpersonal concerns; post-divorce adjustment; relationship with ex-spouse; resolutions of
Child Care, 93
Children,
  abuse of, 81, 105, 106
  and sexual conflicts, 101, 104, 121
  anger of, 9
  attitudes towards, 17
  effect of divorce on, 9, 10
  father's lack of interest in, 83
  mother-child relationships, 78
  post-divorce adjustment of, 81, 90, 100, 101, 109
  positive effect of, 10, 101, 109
  pre-divorce relationship with, 69
  rearing of, 8, 9, 17, 18, 76, 77, 94
  resentment of, 85, 90, 104, 106, 121
  structure, 10, 109
  socialization of, 17
  see single parenting
Child support, 101, 106
  see support, financial
Closure on divorce, 110
Co-custody, 85, 93, 113
  see custody
Cognitive behavior, 122
Communication, 110, 116
Coping mechanisms, 86
Consistency, 105, 106, 112, 113
Control,
  issues of, 87
Counseling
  family, 90, 118
  marriage, 75, 84, 99, 112
  personal, 75, 84, 92
Courtship, 13-14

Index

Crisis
  family, 109
Custodial parent, 100
Custody, 85, 106, 113

Data
  analysis of, 26, 27, 105, 106
Dating, 81, 86, 90, 94, 104
Death
  wishes for, 80
Decision making
  after divorce, 87, 88
  during marriage, 88
Delimitations, 27
Depression, 84, 99, 103, 115, 118
Design of study, 29
  see research design
Determination,
  as a factor in post divorce adjustment, 109
Devastation, 100
Disappointment, 79, 99, 118
Divorce
  adjustment to, 88, 111-14, 118, 122
  areas of, 29
  causes of, 79, 105
  experience of, 1
  identity establishment in, 108, 109, 116, 120
  indications of, 91-96, 107-10, 112, 117
  initiation of, 80, 103, 116-17
  process of, 88, 111-14, 118, 122
  studies of, 1
  see children effect on; identity; infidelity; post-divorce
Differences
  in emergence of central themes, 118
  in resolutions of central themes, 118
  relative, 117
Descriptive statements, 26
Descriptive summaries by subject, 30-64
  see case studies
Disbelief, 80, 99

Ego
  development of, 11
Embarrassment, 84
Employment, 80, 84
Emotional adjustment, 108, 109
Emotional reaction to final separation, 6-7, 83-84, 86, 87, 88, 98, 99, 102, 103, 112, 113, 118, 122
  see anxiety; blame; grieving; guilt; hostility; identity, loss of; loneliness; mourning; rage; rejection; shame; shock
Emotional support, see support systems
Energy, 85
Expectations,
  of identity, 111, 112, 118
  of marriage, 112

Ex-spouse,
  relationship with, 79, 82, 83, 86, 87, 96, 110, 116
  see relationship with ex-spouse

Failure,
  sense of, 67, 80, 99, 105
Family pattern, 12, 109
Family of origin,
  relationship with, 67, 70, 78, 88, 89
Family Unit, 101, 113, 118, 119
Fear, 84, 101, 102, 104, 105, 107
Final separation
  see emotional reaction
Financial concerns, 2, 7-8, 80-81, 84, 85, 93, 101, 106, 110, 114, 122
  see socio-economic factors
Financial,
  impact on divorce, 114-15
  stability, 87
  support, 89, 106
  see child support
Fright, 79, 84

General descriptions of,
  central themes: 79-87
    middle class, 83-87
    working class, 79-87
  pre-divorce conditions: 65-79
    middle class, 71-79
    working clas, 65-71
  resolutions: 87-96
    middle class, 91-96
    working class, 87-91
Grieving
  process of, 6, 99, 102, 103
  degrees of, 6
  symptoms of, 6
  see mourning
Growth,
  personal, 10, 11, 91, 92, 105, 108, 109, 110
  see professional status
Guilt, 79-80, 85, 104, 105, 115, 121

Happiness during marriage, 79, 112
Homosexuality, 73
Humiliation, 72, 81, 84, 101, 102, 106, 114, 121
Husband,
  pre-divorce relation with, 68, 75, 76
  resentment of, 91, 99

Inadequacy
  as parent, 8, 9, 76, 81, 85, 101
  as wife, 6, 95
  feelings of during marriage, 87, 118
Identity, 91, 108, 111
  establishment of, 109, 116, 120
  lack of, 112

loss of, 99, 103
professional, 109, 112
see expectations of marriage
Infidelity, 66, 79, 105, 117
Independence, 12, 88, 108, 109
Initiation of divorce, 80, 84, 103, 105, 112, 116, 122
In-laws, 69, 83
relationship with, 70, 77, 78, 83
see relationships
Inner strengths
definition of, 20
middle class, 74
working class, 66-67
Interpersonal concerns, 1, 10, 11, 90
conflicts of, 104
see dating
Interview, 24, 25, 98
follow up, 25
see research interview
Isolation, 75
Intimacy
conflict of, 104
Intimate relationships after divorce, 90, 92, 94, 107, 108, 116

Jobs, 103
lack of, 81
professional, 84
Joint custody, 106
see co-custody

Love, 73, 74
Loneliness, 80, 86, 92, 99, 103, 104
holidays, 7
Living arrangements
family of origin, 89
friend, 93
independently, 88, 89
Living,
standard of, *see* standard of living
Lived experience,
definition of, 20
Limitations, 27
Lesbians
problems of, 86, 104
relationships, 80, 86, 104
Levels of involvement
definition of, 20, 83
see pre-divorce conditions
Language, 121, 122
impact of, 18, 115

Manipulation, 110
Marriage,
pre-divorce experience of
Middle class, 72-73
Working class, 65-66

models of,
egalitarian, 78, 87, 99, 112
traditional, 66, 83, 99-100, 113, 120
roles in, 14-15, 112
see expectations; pre-divorce conditions; roles; values.
Marriage, reasons for, 100
Men
mistrust of, 90, 102
positive relationship with, 92
see mistrust of men
Middle class,
definition of, 20
Mistrust of men, 90, 110
see men
Mother-child relationships, 78, 113
Mourning, 6, 7, 103, 122
see grieving

Open ended interview
definition of, 20
Open ended questions, 25

Personal growth, 12, 91, 95, 110
see self-esteem
Physical symptoms, 105
Pilot interviews, 24
Population of study, 111, 122
Post divorce
adjustment, 88, 111-14, 118, 119, 122
intimate relationships, 102, 104, 107, 116
social skills, 86
see dating; intimate relationships

Pre-divorce conditions, 2, 9, 10, 26
middle class, 65
studies of, 2
working class, 65-66
see divorce; experience of marriage; inner strengths; relationships; roles; support systems.
Pregnancy, 81
Professional status
impact on post-divorce adjustment, 92, 103, 106, 109, 119, 120
impact on perception of strengths, 74
impact on self-esteem, 94, 95, 109
Property settlements, 93
Psychological terms,
use of, 115

Relationships
see children; husband; family of origin; in-laws; post-divorce; ex-spouse
Reinforcement from ex-spouse, 87
Research
data analysis, 26
case study method, 20-21

Index

design, 20, 29
follow-up interviews, 25
interviews, 24, 25
questions, 3, 97, 98, 104, 107, 108
subjects, 29
see data; interviews; subjects
Rejection, 6, 84, 99, 102, 112
Resentment, 79, 80, 85, 112
of husband, 107
of children, 85, 89, 90, 106-7
see children
Resolution of central themes, 117-23
relative differences, 118-19
objective differences, 119-20
Revenge,
seeking of, 83
Roles
comparison of, 15
in marriage, 2, 14-15, 77, 78, 99, 103, 117
post-divorce, 99, 100, 113, 114
see marriage models

Satisfaction, 95
self, 88
Security, 110
Separation anxiety, 84
Separation,
marital, 117-18
Self-confidence, 95
Self-esteem, 82
changes in, 87, 90-91
during marriage, 82
high, 95
in post divorce adjustment, 117
low, 71, 72, 86, 102, 117
see post-divorce adjustment
Sexual,
abuse, 100
conflicts, 11, 102, 104, 107
demands, 82
dissatisfaction, 73
growth, 13
satisfaction, 99
Sexuality
middle class, 17, 94
working class, 15, 16
see socio-economic impact
Shock, 99, 105, 112, 118
Single parenting, 12
concerns, 5, 8-9, 81, 89-90
conflicts, 9-11
inadequacy as, 8, 81, 100
problems of, 9, 81, 93, 104

responsibilities of, 81, 89, 109, 113
Single person, 85
Socialization of children, 17
Socio-economic
groups, definition of, 21
influences, studies of, 2
impact on
central themes, 1
divorce, 1, 96
marriage, 13-18
post-divorce adjustment, 2, 98
roles in marriage, 2
Social interaction, 5, 10, 11, 118
Social skills, 86
Stability, 108, 109, 113
Standard of living, 85, 93, 103, 106, 114
Statistics, 2
Strengths, 2, 95, 112, 113
see pre-divorce conditions
Stress, 114
Structure,
in lives, 119, 120
Subjects, 29
biographical descriptions, 22-23
middle class, 22-23
working class, 22-23
selection of, 22-23
Suicide, 84, 86
Super mom, 9, 104
Support
financial, 7, 8, 80, 81, 100
see child support
Support systems, 5
agencies, *see* counseling
definitions of, 20
family, 67, 68, 75
friends, 67, 68, 75
husbands, 75
see pre-divorce conditions

Time orientation, 121

Unhappiness, 72, 84, 112

Values in marriage, 96, 113

Welfare, 8, 89, 101, 106, 119
Withdrawal, 86, 94
Women's movement, 108, 113
Working class
definition of, 19
Worthlessness, 102
see self-esteem